BioCritiques

Bloom's BioCritiques

J.D. SALINGER

Edited and with an introduction by
Harold Bloom
Sterling Professor of the Humanities
Yale University

CHELSEA HOUSE PUBLISHERS
Philadelphia

10 9 8 7 6 5 4 3 2

Library of Congress Cataloging-in-Publication Data
applied for

Chelsea House Publishers
1974 Sproul Road, Suite 400
Broomall, PA 19008-0914

http://www.chelseahouse.com

contributing editor: Matt Longabucco

CONTENTS

User's Guide

These volumes are designed to introduce the reader to the life and work of the world's literary masters. Each volume begins with Harold Bloom's essay "The Work in the Writer" and a volume-specific introduction also written by Professor Bloom. Following these unique introductions is an engaging biography that discusses the major life events and important literary accomplishments of the author under consideration.

Furthermore, each volume includes an original critique that not only traces the themes, symbols, and ideas apparent in the author's works, but strives to put those works into a cultural and historical perspectives. In addition to the original critique is a brief selection of significant critical essays previously published on the author and his or her works followed by a concise and informative chronology of the writer's life. Finally, each volume concludes with a bibliography of the writer's works, a list of additional readings, and an index of important themes and ideas.

HAROLD BLOOM

The Work in the Writer

Literary biography found its masterpiece in James Boswell's *Life of Samuel Johnson*. Boswell, when he treated Johnson's writings, implicitly commented upon Johnson as found in his work, even as in the great critic's life. Modern instances of literary biography, such as Richard Ellmann's lives of W. B. Yeats, James Joyce, and Oscar Wilde, essentially follow in Boswell's pattern.

That the writer somehow is in the work, we need not doubt, though with William Shakespeare, writer-of-writers, we almost always need to rely upon pure surmise. The exquisite rancidities of the Problem Plays or Dark Comedies seem to express an extraordinary estrangement of Shakespeare from himself. When we read or attend *Troilus and Cressida* and *Measure for Measure*, we may be startled by particular speeches of Ulysses in the first play, or of Vincentio in the second. These speeches, of Ulysses upon hierarchy or upon time, or of Duke Vincentio upon death, are too strong either for their contexts or for the characters of their speakers. The same phenomenon occurs with Parolles, the military impostor of *All's Well That Ends Well*. Utterly disgraced, he nevertheless affirms: "Simply the thing I am/Shall make me live."

In Shakespeare, more even than in his peers, Dante and Cervantes, meaning always starts itself again through excess or overflow. The strongest of Shakespeare's creatures—Falstaff, Hamlet, Iago, Lear, Cleopatra—have an exuberance that is fiercer than their plays can contain. If Ben Jonson was at all correct in his complaint that "Shakespeare wanted art," it could have been only in a sense that he may not have intended. Where do the personalities of Falstaff or Hamlet touch a limit? What was it in Shakespeare that made the two parts of *Henry IV* and *Hamlet* into "plays unlimited"? Neither Falstaff nor Hamlet will be stopped: their wit, their beautiful, laughing speech, their intensity of being—all these are virtually infinite.

In what ways do Falstaff and Hamlet manifest the writer in the work? Evidently, we can never know, or know enough to answer with any authority. But what would happen if we reversed the question, and asked: How did the work form the writer, Shakespeare?

Of Shakespeare's inwardness, his biography tells us nothing. And yet, to an astonishing extent, Shakespeare created our inwardness. At the least, we can speculate that Shakespeare so lived his life as to conceal the depths of his nature, particularly as he rather prematurely aged. We do not have Shakespeare on Shakespeare, as any good reader of the Sonnets comes to realize: they do not constitute a key that unlocks his heart. No sequence of sonnets could be less confessional or more powerfully detached from the poet's self.

The German poet and universal genius, Goethe, affords a superb contrast to Shakespeare. Of Goethe's life, we know more than everything; I wonder sometimes if we know as much about Napoleon or Freud or any other human being who ever has lived, as we know about Goethe. Everywhere, we can find Goethe in his work, so much so that Goethe seems to crowd the writing out, just as Byron and Oscar Wilde seem to usurp their own literary accomplishments. Goethe, cunning beyond measure, nevertheless invested a rival exuberance in his greatest works that could match his personal charisma. The sublime outrageousness of the Second Part of *Faust*, or of the greater lyric and meditative poems, form a Counter-Sublime to Goethe's own daemonic intensity.

Goethe was fascinated by the daemonic in himself; we can doubt that Shakespeare had any such interests. Evidently, Shakespeare abandoned his acting career just before he composed *Measure for Measure* and *Othello*. I surmise that the egregious interventions by Vincentio and Iago displace the actor's energies into a new kind of mischief-making, a fresh opening to a subtler playwriting-within-the-play.

But what had opened Shakespeare to this new awareness? The answer is the work in the writer, *Hamlet* in Shakespeare. One can go further: it was not so much the play, *Hamlet*, as the character Hamlet, who changed Shakespeare's art forever.

Hamlet's personality is so large and varied that it rivals Goethe's own. Ironically Goethe's Faust, his Hamlet, has no personality at all, and is as colorless as Shakespeare himself seems to have chosen to be. Yet nothing could be more colorful than the Second Part of *Faust*, which is peopled by an astonishing array of monsters, grotesque devils, and classical ghosts.

A contrast between Shakespeare and Goethe demonstrates that in each—but in very different ways—we can better find the work in the person, than we can discover that banal entity, the person in the work. Goethe to many of his contemporaries, seemed to be a mortal god. Shakespeare, so far as we know, seemed an affable, rather ordinary fellow, who aged early and became somewhat withdrawn. Yet Faust, though Mephistopheles battles for his soul, is hardly worth the trouble unless you take him as an idea and not as a person. Hamlet is nearly every-idea-in-one, but he is precisely a personality and a person.

Would Hamlet be so astonishingly persuasive if his father's ghost did not haunt him? Falstaff is more alive than Prince Hal, who says that the devil haunts him in the shape of an old fat man. Three years before composing the final *Hamlet*, Shakespeare invented Falstaff, who then never ceased to haunt his creator. Falstaff and Hamlet may be said to best represent the work in the writer, because their influence upon Shakespeare was prodigious. W.H. Auden accurately observed that Falstaff possesses infinite energy: never tired, never bored, and absolutely both witty and happy until Hal's rejection destroys him. Hamlet too has infinite energy, but in him it is more curse than blessing.

Falstaff and Hamlet can be said to occupy the roles in Shakespeare's invented world that Sancho Panza and Don Quixote possess in Cervantes's. Shakespeare's plays from 1610 on (starting with *Twelfth Night*) are thus analogous to the Second Part of Cervantes's epic novel. Sancho and the Don overtly jostle Cervantes for authorship in the Second Part, even as Cervantes battles against the impostor who has pirated a continuation of his work. As a dramatist, Shakespeare manifests the work in the writer more indirectly. Falstaff's prose genius is revived in the scapegoating of Malvolio by Maria and Sir Toby Belch, while Falstaff's darker insights are developed by Feste's melancholic wit. Hamlet's intellectual resourcefulness, already deadly, becomes poisonous in Iago and in Edmund. Yet we have not crossed into the deeper abysses of the work in the writer in later Shakespeare.

No fictive character, before or since, is Falstaff's equal in self-trust. Sir John, whose delight in himself is contagious, has total confidence both in his self-awareness and in the resources of his language. Hamlet, whose self is as strong, and whose language is as copious, nevertheless distrusts both the self and language. Later Shakespeare is, as it were, much under the influence both of Falstaff and of Hamlet, but they tug him in opposite directions. Shakespeare's own copiousness of language is well-nigh incredible: a vocabulary in excess of twenty-one thousand words, almost eighteen hundred of which he coined himself. And of his word-hoard, nearly half are used only once each, as though the perfect setting for each had been found, and need not be repeated. Love for language and faith in language are Falstaffian attributes. Hamlet will darken both that love and that faith in Shakespeare, and perhaps the Sonnets can best be read as Falstaff and Hamlet counterpointing against one another.

Can we surmise how aware Shakespeare was of Falstaff and Hamlet, once they had played themselves into existence? *Henry IV, Part I* appeared in six quarto editions during Shakespeare's lifetime; *Hamlet* possibly had four. Falstaff and Hamlet were played again and again at the Globe, but Shakespeare knew also that they were being read, and he must have had contact with some of those readers. What would it have been like to discuss Falstaff or Hamlet with one of their early readers (presumably also part of their audience at the Globe), if you were the creator of such demiurges? The question would seem nonsensical to most Shakespeare scholars, but then these days they tend to be either ideologues or moldy figs. How can we recover the uncanniness of Falstaff and of Hamlet, when they now have become so familiar?

A writer's influence upon himself is an unexplored problem in criticism, but such an influence is never free from anxieties. The biocritical problem (which this series attempts to explore) can be divided into two areas, difficult to disengage fully. Accomplished works affect the author's life, and also affect her subsequent writings. It is simpler for me to surmise the effect of *Mrs. Dalloway* and *To the Lighthouse* upon Woolf's late *Between the Acts*, than it is to relate Clarissa Dalloway's suicide and Lily Briscoe's capable endurance in art to the tragic death and complex life of Virginia Woolf.

There are writers whose lives were so vivid that they seem sometimes to obscure the literary achievement: Byron, Wilde, Malraux, Hemingway. But most major Western writers do not live that exuberantly, and the greatest of all, Shakespeare, sometimes appears to have adopted the personal mask of colorlessness. And yet there are heroes of literature who struggled titanically with their own eras—Tolstoy, Milton, Victor Hugo—who nevertheless matter more for their works than their lives.

There are great figures—Emily Dickinson, Wallace Stevens, Willa Cather—who seem to have had so little of the full intensity of life when compared to the vitality of their work, that we might almost speak of the work in the work, rather than even of the work in a person. Emily Brontë might well be the extreme instance of such a visionary, surpassing William Blake in that one regard.

I conclude this general introduction to a series of literary bio-critiques by stating a tentative formula or principle for gauging the many ways in which the work influences the person and her subsequent, later work. Our influence upon ourselves is always related to the Shakespearean invention of self-overhearing, which I have written about in several other contexts. Life, as well as poetry and prose, is overheard rather than simply heard. The writer listens to herself as though she were somebody else, and the will to change begins to operate. The forces that live in us include the prior work we have done, and the dreams and waking visions that evade our dismissals.

HAROLD BLOOM

Introduction

It is now exactly half a century since the publication of *The Catcher in the Rye*. I was then 21, a new graduate student at Yale, and read the book with moderate pleasure, but with little expectation that it would prove to be more than a period piece. Like Salinger's three published volumes of stories, *Catcher* arrived before the advent of the Counterculture in the late 1960s. The Counterculture has become the culture, in the universities, and of the media, and Salinger, a kind of minor prophet of the New Age, is part and parcel of the mediaversity, as we might call it. Salinger's work, sparse but certainly well-written, remains immensely popular with the young, both here and abroad. If his books are period pieces, as I continue to believe, they have already survived into a second period. Holden Caulfield is not Huckleberry Finn, but nobody else is either, though we are now in the novelistic era of Philip Roth, Don De Lillo, Cormac McCarthy, and (if he is a novelist, and not an epic prose-poet) Thomas Pynchon. Salinger, growing up between the two World Wars, and a combat veteran of the Normandy invasion and the Battle of the Bulge, like Norman Mailer began as a disciple of Hemingway, but with an admixture of Scott Fitzgerald, in Salinger's case. The prose of the *Catcher* and of the stories is a skillful fusion of Hemingway and Fitzgerald. Is Salinger then, like John Updike, a minor fiction-writer with a major style?

Since Salinger, for whatever reason, has chosen mythic isolation, his legend remains curiously lively. There is hardly enough published work to speculate upon the work in the writer, or Salinger's influence upon himself.

The saga of the Glass family is told (more or less) in the three short story volumes, *Nine Stories* (1953), *Franny and Zooey* (1961), and *Raise High the Roof Beam, Carpenters and Seymour: an Introduction* (1963). Adroit as almost all of these 13 stories are, they contain no deep surprises for readers of *The Catcher in the Rye*.

Perhaps Salinger, after the immediate success of *Catcher*, feared he could not equal it, or more likely, his contemplative obsession with Eastern religion turned him towards a noncommunicative inwardness. The stories remain popular with the same audience that sustains *Catcher*, but they in no way demonstrate any advance or development in Salinger's narrative art. Seymour—their spiritual center—is rather hard to take, if you are not an adoring Glass sibling.

What constitutes Salinger's achievement is Holden Caulfield, who oddly may yet outlive his book, since what matters most about him is his stance or attitude. He is Huck Finn's disciple, and not David Copperfield's, and in Huck's mode Holden blends an idealistic good will with a profound suspicion of all adult authorities.

Huck is haunted by the realistic fear that his ghastly, murderous, alcoholic Pap might show up again. Holden is shadowed by his brother's death, and is himself afraid of death, of sex, and of the partly conscious conviction that maturity is deathly. There are no parents or teachers available to guide Holden, since he could not accept them anyway.

Whether Holden is a fully realized consciousness or primarily just a narrative voice is disputable. The voice is desperate, and heading towards psychic breakdown, as though having turned 16 constituted the pragmatic end. Love, for Holden, is possible only for Phoebe, his 10-year-old sister. Watching her, in the rain, Holden evokes Nick Carraway at Gatsby's funeral, and Frederic Henry walking away after Catherine's death, in *A Farewell to Arms*.

Holden's darkest moment is when he cites as his paradigm the New Testament's Legion, who is demon-infested, mentally ill, tomb-haunting: "If you want to know the truth, the guy I like best in the Bible, next to Jesus, was that lunatic and all, that lived in the tombs." Legion's madness is barely evaded by Holden, who is able to survive because of his wistful dream of himself as a Jesus-like savior of children: "What I have to do, I have to catch everybody if they start to go over the cliff—."

To speculate that Holden may survive his book is only to imply that Salinger has made two myths: Holden Caulfield and J.D. Salinger. Of the two, Holden is the more attractive, but then literature has all the advantages over life. Holden always will be 16. Salinger, now 82, has demonstrated that he too is a survivor, and on his own terms.

NORMA JEAN LUTZ

Biography of J.D. Salinger

HORRORS OF WAR

On June 6, 1944, the Allied Forces launched the largest military sea and air invasion known to humankind. World War II had raged in Europe for more than two years before America entered the war in 1941 after the bombing of Pearl Harbor. The powerful Nazi forces often seemed to prevail in Europe, but the massive D-Day invasion hoped to change all that. The attack was scheduled for June 5, but a storm caused General Dwight D. Eisenhower to postpone it for one day. Thousands of ships, planes, and troops sat poised in Southern England awaiting the signal to launch. The Allied forces mainly comprised British, Canadian, and American soldiers, sailors, and airmen.

One American soldier in the 12th Infantry Regiment of the Fourth Division, Jerome David Salinger, had arrived in England the previous March. Stationed in Tiverton, Devon, England, he received extensive training in counterintelligence operations. While Salinger didn't know it at the time, this kind of training would prove necessary in the Allied invasion of occupied Europe.

On the morning of D-Day, 25-year-old Salinger found himself in an amphibian troop mover that was transporting him and his comrades across the English Channel to Utah Beach in Normandy. Even with the surprise element of the invasion, the Germans were putting up massive resistance. The men hunkered down in the troop movers; they could do nothing but sit and wait as the sounds of bombing and gunfire grew in intensity.

The landing had been timed for low tide to expose underwater ramps, steel gates, barbed wire, and welded steel rails—all rigged with mines placed by Hitler's army. Of the five landing locations, Omaha Beach was the most heavily defended. More than 4,000 men died to secure the area. The more fortunate Fourth Division stormed Utah Beach, missing their mark by 2,000 yards and meeting lighter resistance than those at Omaha. When the landing craft hit the shore and the men piled out, Salinger waded out into the cold waters and onto the beach—this was his introduction to the gruesome realities of war.

The supreme commander of the invasion, Brigadier General Theodore Roosevelt Jr. chose to land reinforcements and supplies in the same spot. Because of lighter resistance, they secured the beachhead within hours, and the Fourth Division moved inland to make contact with the airborne divisions already scattered across the front.

While the uniform he wore symbolized unity and conformity, J.D. Salinger was different from the other men in his outfit. Instead of writing home to his mom, wife, or sweetheart, Salinger spent much of his time sending letters, postcards, and manuscripts to magazine editors. As he went about the business of liberating Europe and interrogating German prisoners, Salinger wrote short stories and mailed them off regularly. Eager to make the most of every writing opportunity he often kept a typewriter in his jeep. In a letter to writing instructor, Whit Burnett, Salinger wrote, "Am still writing whenever I can find the time and an unoccupied foxhole." An Army buddy remembered Salinger crouched beneath a table typing away while the area was under attack.

By the time Salinger arrived in Europe, he had already seen his short stories published in *Story* magazine and the *Saturday Evening Post*. These early stories, basically patriotic references to war and battle, glorified the need to fight and kill to make things right. His experience in real war would permanently change that tone.

Before the war, J.D. Salinger had been known as a loner. He was often thought of as being somewhat arrogant—a man who needed no one. He grew up around New York's posh Park Avenue, the son of a wealthy Jewish father, but he never fit in with the other kids. The months spent in the worst fighting of the war would be the first time he ever felt the need to trust and depend on others. The experience, however, proved to be mostly temporary. At heart, he was still aloof. As one war buddy remembered:

We worked together as a pair on several occasions. I didn't think of him as a friend. I was from poor people and he was from rich people. We generally got along on a live-and-let-live basis. In my opinion, he would look down on me and I sometimes thought he was a little belligerent. When I felt I didn't agree with him, I would just walk away. There was no animosity, but he was a kind of lone wolf.

As the regiment pressed into France toward Cherbourg, Salinger's job was to destroy communications by shutting down telephone lines and taking over post offices in the villages and towns along the way. "They would then begin interrogating the hundreds of prisoners who were rounded up in the so-called Civilian Cage: on the look-out here for collaborators and for German army deserters in civilian clothing."

By August, the troops moved toward Paris, where wildly enthusiastic Parisians turned out to greet them. Crowds surged into the streets and swarmed around the tanks and trucks, shouting "*Merci! Merci!*" As one British soldier reported, "the pent-up delirious crowds just wanted to touch us, to feel if we were real." The civilians handed out long-hoarded bottles of fine wine, flowers, and fruit to the soldiers in an attempt to express their deep gratitude. This was the first joyful moment for the battle-weary U.S. soldiers since they landed at Normandy.

The triumphant march did not mean the city was totally free. Approximately 20,000 Germans were still holed up in Paris, and subsequent house-to-house fighting netted 3,000 Germans killed and more than 10,000 prisoners taken. J.D. was most assuredly involved in this campaign. Still, with all this heavy fighting, his thoughts seldom strayed from his writing.

During this time, noted author Ernest Hemingway was serving as a war correspondent in Paris and had set up shop at the Ritz Hotel. He was there when the troops arrived. When Salinger found this out, he grabbed a copy of the *Saturday Evening Post* containing his story, "Last Day of the Last Furlough," invited a buddy to come along, and headed for the Ritz. The magazine story was about two families caught up in the tragedies of war, the type of story that would appeal to Hemingway. During their first meeting, Salinger seemed enthralled to talk to such a successful author. In a letter to a friend, he described Hemingway as "modest" and "not big-shotty." This very type of fawning over celebrities Salinger detested when he later became famous.

After a short stay in Paris, Salinger's regiment was deployed to the Huertgen Forest. Here was fought one of the most savage and useless battles of the entire war. The forest covered roughly 50 square miles along the

German-Belgium border. It was a somber, gloomy place even without the tragedy of war. For soldiers attempting to make their way through this enemy-infested area, it became a living nightmare. "It was like a green cave, always dripping water, the firs interlocked their lower limbs so that everyone had to stoop all the time.... Add to this gloom the mixture of sleet, snow, rain, cold, fog and almost knee-deep mud."

At age 25, J.D. Salinger ranked as an "old man," since most of the unseasoned soldiers around him were barely 18 or 19 years old. Thousands of these young GIs were sent into the dark enemy-entrenched forest. They faced an onslaught of machine guns, rifles, and mortars, in addition to being caught in dense minefields.

Salinger's Fourth Division followed on the heels of the Twenty-eighth Division, which had been nearly annihilated. These D-Day veterans were once again being asked to pour out their lifeblood. Between November 7 and December 3, the Fourth lost over 7,000 men in the Huertgen Forest. In a battle that dragged on for months, Salinger saw many of his friends and comrades killed and wounded in action—a haunting vision for any soldier. Combat veterans of this battle later testified that only on the rarest of occasions did they see any officer above the rank of captain or any officer from the staff during the hostilities. Those making battle decisions failed to survey the area. Therefore, orders to continue the battle came from officers who did not know or understand the terrain. It would later be determined that the entire battle of Huertgen Forest, which claimed the lives of more than 24,000 American soldiers, was the result of bureaucratic mistakes.

After Huertgen, there is reason to believe that Salinger was in the thick of the Battle of the Bulge. The Fourth Division held against the Germans, enabling Allied forces in the south to reorganize. And so the Allies won the battle for Luxembourg on December 26, 1945.

Back home, friends of Salinger knew generally of his whereabouts and wondered about his safety. Late in 1944, he sent V-mail to his friend, Elizabeth Murray, describing the brighter moments such as the liberation of Paris and telling about the stories he'd still been able to write. Still, he said that he was more than ready to come home. On December 27, Whit Burnett noted in a memo: "Salinger well. Letter and phone to his mother. December 17."

These wartime experiences had a dramatic effect on Salinger as the next story he wrote marked a fundamental shift in his thinking about war. "A Boy in France," appeared in the *Saturday Evening Post* on March 31, 1945. All the glory of war had faded, as the story honed in on one lonely GI in a foxhole in France longing to go home. This story had a definite tone of anguish and despair.

By the time the Germans surrendered to the Allied forces, Salinger was suffering from exhaustion and confusion and had problems coping with everyday life. He became one of the many GIs who suffered from "battle fatigue." In July, he checked into an Army hospital in Nuremberg, where he was diagnosed as having suffered a nervous breakdown.

In a later story entitled, "The Stranger," Salinger poignantly expressed the loss of war. The main character, a war veteran named Babe, is listening to a Bakewell Howard jazz record playing "Fat Boy" and hears in it:

> The music of the irrecoverable years, the little, unhistorical, pretty good years when all the dead boys in the 12th Regiment had been living and cutting in on other dead boys on lost dance floors: the years when no one who could dance worth a damn had ever heard of Cherbourg, of St.-Lo or Huertgen Forest or Luxembourg.

In Salinger's mind, there would forever be a separation between those who knew firsthand about battle and those who simply read about it.

GROWING UP JEWISH

The family of J.D. Salinger was decidedly Jewish at a time when it was not popular to be Jewish in America. In the mid-1880s, J.D.'s grandfather, Simon Salinger, served as rabbi for a congregation in Louisville, Kentucky. His true desire, however, was to be a physician. Simon requested permission from his congregation to be released to return to medical school. Permission was granted and, with a wife and five children, Simon changed his life's direction. He completed medical school and spent the remainder of his life serving others as a noted physician.

Because the Salingers kept few records about their heritage, their genealogy has many holes. It is not known where Simon's son, Solomon, fit in the family birth order, nor how the family happened to migrate from Kentucky to Chicago. Perhaps Solomon moved to Chicago alone before he married and had children.

What is known is that Solomon met and married a young woman named Marie Jillich, a Catholic girl from County Cork, Ireland, who wore her waist-length auburn hair flowing free and turned heads wherever she went. Solomon met Marie at a county fair somewhere near Marie's parents' farm. It was love at first sight. The tall, handsome 22-year-old city man subsequently eloped with the 17-year-old farm girl.

Marie's family instantly disowned her and never spoke to her again. This rift caused the Salinger children to grow up knowing nothing about their maternal grandparents. Having lost her own family, it is believed Marie must have wanted very much to fit into Solomon's Jewish family, as she changed her name from Marie to the biblical name Miriam. Rejection may also have come from Solomon's family because Jewish families certainly did not smile upon mixed marriages. However, Solomon's mother eventually accepted Miriam and came to love her as one of her own.

In their early years as a married couple living in Chicago, Solomon operated a movie theater, and Miriam helped out by working at the ticket booth and the concession stand. The couple had a daughter in 1911 and named her Doris. Doris remembered their family as being at a disadvantage financially. She later commented, "Of all those Jews in the business at that time, Daddy was the only one who didn't make it big." That situation was destined to change.

Later, Solomon hired on with the J.D. Hoffman Company, an importer of European cheeses and meats. Hoffman sold products under the names of Hofco Family Swiss Cuts and Hofco Baby Goudas. It was a business for which Solomon was more suited. He showed enough promise to be moved to New York City to become general manager of Hoffman's New York operation.

In the ensuing years, Miriam suffered two miscarriages. When she became pregnant again, she contracted pneumonia during the sixth month. Her doctors left her with little hope that the baby would make it. Jerome David Salinger proved the doctors wrong, making his way into the world at the New York Nursery and Child's Hospital on New Year's Day, 1919.

The family immediately nicknamed the baby Sonny, and his mother doted on him. Sister Doris attributed the overabundance of affection to the fact that boys were very special in Jewish families. Miriam's doting might also have been a result of having lost two babies, and very nearly losing Sonny. Whichever it was, Doris stated that in their mother's eyes, ". . . he [Sonny] could do no wrong." Then Doris added, "I thought he was perfect too."

At the time of Sonny's birth, the Salingers lived at 3681 Broadway, but within the year they moved to 113th Street in a predominantly Jewish neighborhood. The years following WWI were difficult times for Jews in the United States. Anti-Semitic feelings caused many Jews to change their names to rid themselves of any Jewish connotation. Such respected magazines as the *Saturday Evening Post* joined in the onslaught, calling Jews from Poland (such as Solomon Salinger), "human parasites . . . mongoloids not fit to govern themselves." Classified ads in the newspapers made it clear that Jews were not welcome to apply for even the most menial jobs. This was the world in which Sonny Salinger grew up.

In Sonny's Upper West Side neighborhood, more than 50 percent of the population was Jewish, boasting 10 synagogues in the area. Such a community made it more comfortable to be Jewish despite the attitudes of the rest of the country. Unlike some of their more devout neighbors, the Salingers did not attend religious services, and in fact, they celebrated Christmas. Neither Doris nor Sonny would know until much later that their mother was Catholic and that they were only half-Jewish. When they learned the truth, it came as a shock. As Doris later told J.D.'s daughter, Peggy, "It wasn't nice to be half-Jewish in those days. It was no asset to be Jewish either, but at least you belonged somewhere."

Until eighth grade, Sonny attended schools in which most of his classmates were Jewish. Even though the Salingers made several moves during these grammar-school years, Sonny went to public schools, and in his daily life he was immersed in the Jewish culture.

Sonny was described during these years as a "solemn," and "polite" boy, who didn't mind spending time alone. His grades were average except for math, which was poor. At age 11, Sonny had an opportunity to attend summer camp away from the crowded city. At Camp Wigwam in Harrison, Maine, Sonny had a number of new and interesting experiences, one of which was being voted as the camp's most popular actor. Drama would become a focal point in Sonny's young life.

Even though it was the beginning of the Great Depression, Solomon's success slowly grew until in 1932 the family was able to move to Park Avenue. Gone were the friendly Jewish faces and familiar Jewish customs; gone were the kosher shops and synagogues. Sonny had celebrated his bar mitzvah a year before the move, which was when he and Doris found out that their mother was not Jewish, but Catholic. The impact on Sonny of this shocking truth can never be measured. Suffice it to say that the subject of being half-Jewish appears in many of his stories.

As if the move and this new revelation about his mother were not enough, Sonny was enrolled in a private school called McBurney, part of the Young Men's Christian Association—yet another life-changing event during a volatile time in his life. During the enrollment interview at the prep school, Sonny flippantly stated that he was interested in two subjects: "drama and tropical fish," demonstrating a hint of his defensive attitude. Although he must have felt out of place at the elite school, Sonny did become involved in several activities. He managed the fencing team, became a reporter for the school paper (the *McBurneian*), and acted in two plays, taking the female parts in each one.

A write-up in the school paper about a play called *Mary's Ankle* noted, "Some think Jerome Salinger . . . gave the best performance." In another play, *Jonesy*, Sonny played the part of a well-meaning mother, and again the paper described him as "very good in dramatics." We also learn from a McBurney report that he was "good in public speaking." These incidents certainly indicate that as a boy, Salinger showed an innate talent for drama. His father, however, opposed any talk about a career in acting. As many successful businessmen-fathers did during this era, Solomon insisted that his son follow him into the business.

One of his friends said that Sonny "wanted to do unconventional things. For hours, no one in the family knew where he was or what he was doing; he just showed up for meals. He was a nice boy, but he was the kind of kid who, if you wanted to have a card game, wouldn't join in."

By the spring of 1934, Sonny had flunked out of the fine private school. A note on his transcript stated that the boy had been rather "hard-hit by [adolescence] his last year with us." It also stated that while Jerome Salinger had plenty of ability, he did not know the meaning of the word "industry." That summer, he was placed in the Manhassat School to try to improve his grades. That, too, became a disaster. The next step was to send Sonny off to a military school to be toughened up. Valley Forge Military School near Wayne, Pennsylvania, emphasized sports and military subjects over academics. Again, the shock of high expectations and a sudden change in setting must have been difficult for him. As Salinger's daughter Peggy noted in her book, *Dream Catcher*, this area of Pennsylvania was rated by the U.S. Army War Board as the heart of anti-Semitism in America. Salinger's older sister Doris said that the anti-Semitism at the school was "hell on Sonny." The circumstances at the school created yet another reason for young Salinger to put up and maintain a defensive wall and to keep his distance from the other boys.

The nickname "Sonny" was now left behind as a childhood thing. Salinger did not like his first name, David sounded too Jewish, and J.D. seemed too formal. His new name, he decided, would be Jerry. Friends and family were informed about this change, though his sister Doris continued to refer to her younger brother as Sonny.

By his second year at Valley Forge, Jerry appeared to be fitting in as well as could be expected. He became literary editor of the class yearbook, *Crossed Sabres*, and was virtually the author of the entire book, which left behind a clear history of his two years at the school. Other activities were Glee Club, Aviation Club, French Club, and the Non-Commissioned Officers Club. Dearest to Jerry's heart was being a devoted member of the Mask and Spur Dramatic Club—his love for drama and acting endured.

Jerry never quite matched the rebelliousness of Holden Caulfield, yet he still found his share of mischief. At times, he and a friend snuck out across the campus toward a nearby estate belonging to an heir to the Campbell Soup fortune where they slipped inside the gates and enjoyed nighttime swims in the pool. At other times Jerry would sneak out before dawn, run into town and eat breakfast, and return safely before reveille.

For the most part, Jerry appeared to obey the rules and even went so far as to improve his grades. He never did appreciate or fit in with the military aspects of the school. Richard Gonder, his senior roommate, later commented that Jerry poked fun at the "silly routines" of the school.

> The school in those days was run on a strictly military basis—up at six, endless formations, marching from one activity to another, meals and classes at set hours, taps at ten. Jerry did everything he could do not to earn a cadet promotion, which he considered childish and absurd.

In addition to his love of drama, Salinger discovered a deep love for writing while at Valley Forge. A friend from school remembered him writing by flashlight at night under the bedcovers. He later broke out of that limited routine when his insatiable thirst for creating stories had forced him to write every spare minute.

Salinger always thought of himself as an outsider even though he appeared to fit in. In addition to being Jewish, he was the more sophisticated big-city kid, who attended Broadway plays and read *New Yorker* magazine. This obviously led the way to reverse snobbery. He often bragged about how he planned to go to Hollywood and make "big money." He wrote his own class prediction for the yearbook and said that he would be "writing four-act melodramas for the Boston Philharmonic Orchestra."

Salinger emerged from Valley Forge confident that he would become a writer—fully committed to the pursuit of artistic excellence. As his friend Richard said, "I liked him immensely. I enjoyed his wit and humor. He was so sure of himself as far as his writing went. He knew he was good."

SEEKING DIRECTION

Salinger's grades improved at military school, but he was still barely passing. Poor grades combined with the fact that many universities were still not accepting Jews as students or professors made getting into college difficult. All of which may explain in part Salinger's revulsion for what he later referred to as Ivy League snobbery. Despite such hinderances, Salinger settled on New York University's Washington Square College. The university's Manhattan location in the heart of Greenwich Village along with its acceptance of Jews would have been of significant appeal to Salinger. Here he enrolled in basic freshman courses, but the creative energies displayed at Valley Forge were absent from his first year of college.

Complicating Salinger's return to New York was his dismay at having to live at home again. Herbert Kauffman, a friend from military school, stayed in the Salinger home for a time and remembered heated arguments between Jerry and his father. However, Sol was not the belligerent one; Kauffman said that it was Jerry who was sarcastic and unfair to his father. In the midst of the Great Depression, Soloman felt that the profession of neither writer nor actor would do his son any good. Nonetheless, Jerry and his friend Herb made a stab at being actors, going from theater to theater hoping for a big break. When nothing panned out, Jerry either agreed to, or was pressured to, accompany his father to Europe to learn the family business.

While Soloman and Jerry probably visited Paris and London; most of their time was spent in Vienna, where Jerry worked on his German and French speaking abilities. He lived in the Jewish sector of Vienna in the home of a Jewish family whom he came to love. Their teenage daughter became a special focus of Salinger's affections. Salinger's daughter Peggy recalled her father speaking of the family with great affection. Tragically, every member of this particular family was killed in German concentration camps during the war. Austria fell to the Nazis only a few months after Salinger's visit. The knowledge that the family he loved was in mortal danger must have had a profound effect upon young Salinger.

From Vienna, Salinger traveled to Poland for a hands-on experience with the Hoffman's meat business. In a 1944 issue of *Story* Magazine, Salinger described this experience in Poland:

> I was supposed to apprentice myself to the Polish ham business.
> They finally dragged me off to Bydgoszcz for a couple of months,
> where I slaughtered pigs, wagoned through the snow with the
> big slaughtermaster who was determined to entertain me by
> firing his shot-gun at sparrows, lightbulbs, fellow employees . . .

Salinger would later say that he detested every aspect of the slaughtering of pigs. What happened between father and son on the voyage home is unknown, but nothing more was ever said about Jerry becoming a part of his father's business. Back in America, Salinger was still a young man with no formal education and seemingly no occupation.

He decided to once again take a stab at college. He enrolled at Ursinus College, a small school in rural Collegeville, Pennsylvania. The school was sponsored by the Evangelical and Reformed Church, and was in close proximity to Valley Forge Military Academy. Salinger started classes in the fall of 1938.

Salinger made his mark at Ursinus by being the in-the-know world traveler who told fascinating stories about his jaunts abroad. In contrast, many of the students at Ursinus were fresh out of high schools from the small surrounding communities. Salinger again found some of those creative energies joining the writing staff of the *Ursinus Weekly*, the school newspaper. At first, as drama critic, he reviewed three of the school plays in which he almost woodenly said a good word about every player. The tone of his regular column called, "The Skipped Diploma: Musing of a Social Soph" was much different. The column was used to put forth a knowing tone of "I've seen it all," while making arrogant digs at academic life. In his movie reviews, he belittled handsome romantic male actors and raved about Mickey Rooney and the Marx Brothers.

One fellow student remarked: "I do remember him and I remember him because it is my impression that he was not close to anyone—students or professors. Indeed, my recollection is he was pretty much a loner." Yet another classmate commented that Salinger had no friends or companions. "Jerry came from New York and looked on the college and students with disdain. He seemed so dissatisfied. . . . He never smiled, gave a friendly greeting, or responded to overtures of acceptance. His manner was nasty. His remarks, if any, were caustic."

However, girls felt differently about this handsome boy full of worldly ways. One special friend named Frances Thierolf remembered:

> When this handsome, suave, and sophisticated New Yorker in the black Chesterfield coat (complete with velvet collar) hit the campus in 1938, we had never seen anything quite like it. . . .
>
> Most of the girls were mad about him at once—including me—and the boys held him slightly in awe with a trace of envy thrown in. . . . He declared openly that he would one day produce the Great American Novel. Jerry and I became special friends, mostly, I am sure, because I was the only one who believed he would do it.

The name Franny became a favorite for Salinger to use in his stories. It is further speculated that the Salinger's character Franny Glass is named after Frances Glassmoyer —Frances Thierolf's married name.

While Salinger spent only one semester at Ursinus, his daughter would later remark that she never heard her father say a negative word about the school. He did not flunk out, but he was restless. A fellow student, Charles Steinmetz, who was in an English class with Salinger recalled, ". . . Jerry didn't enjoy the English class because it wasn't what he wanted. He told me once, 'I'm not satisfied. This is not what I want.'" On another occaision Salinger told Steinmetz, "Charlie, I have to be a writer. I have to. Going here is not going to help me." When Salinger made his decision to leave, he told no one. Fellow student Richard Deitzler recalls, "One day he was there, going to classes, writing for the school newspaper, telling stories to his dormmates. The next day he was gone." Once again Salinger found himself living under his parents' roof.

During the previous summer, Salinger and a friend from Valley Forge, William Faison, traveled together to William's sister's home near Point Pleasant, New Jersey. The sister, Elizabeth Murray—12 years older than her brother—became a good friend to Salinger. Elizabeth appeared to take an interest in his writing and offered to help edit his work.

When Salinger returned to New York from Ursinus, Elizabeth met him there at a place called Jumble Shop, in Greenwich Village, where they spent hours talking about his work. Elizabeth's daughter, Gloria Murray, recalled that her mother cared about Salinger:

> She thought he was a little self-absorbed. She also thought that he used her as a sounding board. When he read the stories to her, she flattered him because she did think they were interesting and rather comical. He read the stories to her because he thought she understood his writing. He was anxious for her comments and she was supportive.

Not only did Elizabeth encourage Jerry in his writing, she steered him to other good writers. At that time, he had never heard of F. Scott Fitzgerald, but upon reading *The Great Gatsby*, he became fascinated with the author. Encouragement from Elizabeth came at a time when Salinger needed it desperately. His parents were unsympathetic, and he'd received nothing but rejection slips in his efforts to be published. Gloria Murray agrees:

> My mother was the one who gave that vital encouragement to Salinger. Their relationship never became anything more than that—her supporting him as a fledgling artist. But what a gesture my mother made to him. I do believe he was aware of the importance and selflessness of the gesture at the time, too.

Salinger knew he needed more than courses in English, composition, and literature. He needed specific guidance in his writing. He found that guidance in a writing class offered at Columbia University taught by short story writer, Whit Burnett. While Burnett's class was well attended, he was better known for his position as the editor of the literary journal *Story*, which he founded in 1931. As an editor, Burnett had an eye for promising talent, publishing the first works of such authors as Tennessee Williams, Truman Capote, and Carson McCullers.

Salinger signed up for Burnett's noncredit course in the spring of 1939. For the first semester, he sat back and simply listened. Here was a class that held no pressure. He could sit quietly and absorb all that went on without any thoughts of flunking or passing. Burnett recalled that first semester:

> There was one dark-eyed, thoughtful young man who sat through one semester of a class in writing without taking notes, seemingly not listening, looking out the window. A week or so before the semester ended, he suddenly came to life. He began to write. Several stories seemed to come from his typewriter at once, and most of these were published. The young man was J.D. Salinger.

Burnett was duly impressed with the polished, stylish, and even sophisticated stories. When Salinger submitted one to *Story* magazine entitled, "The Young Folks," Burnett quickly accepted it. The story was written mostly in dialogue with very little interior monologue, sounding more like a play than a short story. Dialogue would always be one of Salinger's strong points. Another aspect of this story that would become a hallmark in Salinger's writings was an ongoing obsession with the thinking and actions of young people.

Salinger's letters from this time period reveal that he was terribly excited about his first sale. When writing the contributor's notes for the magazine, he stated in his cover letter that he had "butterflies in his stomach" and that he was "overwhelmed" by the event. The story appeared in the March-April, 1940, issue of *Story*.

Success came to Salinger a second time in 1940 when he was published in a college literary magazine, the *University of Kansas City Review*. As far as we know, this was his only sale to a literary publication.

Consequently, having been published in Burnett's well-known and closely watched magazine, Salinger was approached by a literary agent. He signed on with Harold Ober's agency and was assigned to a woman named Dorothy Olding. The two would go on to have a long and profitable business association. Having his own literary agent gave Salinger's self-confidence a needed boost.

The constraints of living with his parents must have been trying for Salinger, yet there is no indication that he was ever gainfully employed or that he even looked for a job during his time with them. Instead, he spent the summer of 1940 traveling to Canada and Cape Cod. While he was away, Salinger dropped newsy postcards to Whit Burnett in an obvious attempt to maintain an ongoing relationship. Salinger later built up an intense mistrust of editors and disdained almost any type of author-editor relationship.

In part, the reasoning behind his summer trip was to get away and think more clearly about the direction of his life. This lack of direction was noted in one of Salinger's post cards on which he considered the option of becoming an actor. However, when he returned to New York in the fall of 1940, the decision had been made. He was prepared to throw his energies into writing.

Short Story Writer

In the 1930s and 1940s, a writer could make a decent living writing short stories for popular magazines. Finances were tight and entertainment choices were slim, so people read magazine stories as a form of inexpensive entertainment. Magazines—some with circulations up to two million—paid very good prices for stories. Acoording to some sources, "*Collier's*, *Liberty*, and *The Saturday Evening Post* were paying around $2,000 (about $26,500 in today's dollars) for a short story." Salinger hoped to take his career in this direction, with the ultimate goal of graduating from the common slicks to the more sophisticated magazines such as *Esquire* and the *New Yorker*. With his direction clear, he completed a number of short stories at an incredible rate.

In the fall of 1940, Salinger cast his vote in the national election for then-president, Franklin Delano Roosevelt, who was running for a second term. Roosevelt won a landslide victory over Wendell Wilkie and became the leader to guide the country through the tumultuous years that lay ahead. The escalating war in Europe was a cause for concern for every American. With that in mind, Salinger wrote stories about the lives of people in the military, realizing that this popular subject made salable copy. He was right, his *short* short story entitled, "The Hang of It," was sold to *Collier's* and appeared in the July 12, 1941, issue. It was Salinger's first byline in a national magazine. Unlike the stories he would write later, his first works were specifically slanted to the popular magazines—they were designed and written to sell. Meanwhile, he continued submitting to the *New Yorker*, but to no avail.

During the summer of 1941, Salinger and his friend, William Faison, spent time in New Jersey with Faison's sister, Elizabeth Murray. While there, Jerry was introduced to a family friend, Oona O'Neill, daughter of famous playwright, Eugene O'Neill.

Oona was 15 years old at the time and had been reared by her mother with little or no input or support from her famous father. She attended exclusive all-girls schools, where she socialized with other girls from wealthy families, such as the Vanderbilts. Oona possessed an almost haunting loveliness—the type that turned every head when she walked into a room. In a future decade, another lovely debutante by the name of Jacqueline Bouvier (Kennedy) would be compared to Oona O'Neill.

Elizabeth's daughter, Gloria, noted that Salinger also succumbed to O'Neill's stunning beauty. "He fell for her on the spot. He was taken with her beauty and impressed that she was the daughter of Eugene O'Neill. She seemed to be impressed that he was a writer, too." Back in New York, the two began seeing one another regularly, attending plays and movies together. Twenty-two-year-old Salinger had fallen in love with a fifteen-year-old schoolgirl.

In the fall of 1941, Jerry's next big sale was to *Esquire* magazine, a story about love, "The Heart of the Broken Story." Also in 1941 Salinger penned a story starring a character named Holden Caulfield, a young boy from an affluent neighborhood and family who was weary of everything in his life. "Slight Rebellion Off Madison" expressed the exasperation of a boy who wanted to run away and live in the woods with his girlfriend, Sally. It became evident that Salinger knew he'd found a strong believable character. At about the same time as these stories, Jerry Salinger started using his initials as his byline. Friends and family continued to know him as Sonny and Jerry, but the world would come to know him as J.D. Salinger.

When Salinger received word that the *New Yorker* magazine had accepted "Slight Rebellion," he was overjoyed. His elation, however, was short-lived. Before the story could be scheduled for publication, the Japanese attacked Pearl Harbor on December 7, 1941, after which Congress declared war on Japan. Under the circumstances, the editors at the *New Yorker* felt that the story of a rebellious teenager would be inappropriate for the moment. The timing was wrong.

During this time, Salinger and a friend were briefly employed aboard a Caribbean ocean liner, the *MS Kungsholm*. The two young men worked as activity directors organizing games and dancing with the single women. Whether or not they were actually involved in the entertainment aspect of the cruise is not known. Even though it was a brief sojourn, the experience would stay with Salinger for years because it was the closest he ever came to the world of entertainment.

Before the war, Salinger had attempted to join the U.S. Army but was turned away because he had a mild heart condition. Later, as the war progressed, mild heart conditions meant very little. The government eventually redefined classifications, making Salinger eligible to join. In the spring of 1942, Salinger's number came up. He first reported to Fort Dix, New Jersey, on April 27, 1942, and later was sent to Fort Monmouth, New Jersey, where he received instruction with the Signal Corps. Salinger's experiences as a boy in military school may have helped him adjust to life in the Army. He soon applied for Officer Candidate School with a glowing letter of recommendation from Colonel Baker of Valley Forge Military Academy. He was accepted but never called.

Salinger's next transfer took the New York boy into the Deep South, where he was assigned to the post of Army Aviation Cadets instructor at the Army Air Force Basic Flying School in Bainbridge, Georgia. He never learned to enjoy the South, which he saw as slow, sticky, and full of bugs. However, during his stay, he kept up an ongoing correspondence with O'Neill. His absence from her only convinced him of how much he loved her.

With much of his time devoted to serving in the military, Salinger found little time to write, but stories submitted earlier continued to be published. While he was stationed in Georgia, Salinger received a copy of *Story* magazine, which contained his short story, "The Long Debut of Lois Taggert." In this and other writings, Salinger filled the pages with impetuous, mistaken marriage unions. Phony, empty-headed debutantes appear as girls with a need to be punished. Even cruelty and abuse sometimes found their way into his stories.

While Salinger was serving, O'Neill and her friend, Carole Marcus, decided to move to the West Coast. At the time, Marcus was dating writer and playwright, William Saroyan—the couple later later married. Marcus remembered the letters O'Neill received from Salinger, some of which were more than 15 pages long. However, it was also during this time that O'Neill was introduced to Charles Chaplin, the famous film star and director. Chaplin, known for his comedic roles in silent films, was 54 when he and O'Neill first met. The two immediately became an item, and news of the romance appeared in gossip columns in all the major newspapers. The couple married on June 16, 1943. When Oona's father heard about the marriage, he immediately disowned his daughter and the two never spoke again.

Letters to Whit Burnett indicated that Salinger suffered greatly over the loss of O'Neill. Brokenhearted or not, Salinger managed to continue writing. The summer of 1943 brought the publication of another of his stories in the *Saturday Evening Post*. He had hopes that this story, "The Varioni Brothers," would be purchased by Hollywood, a dream that never materialized. By fall, his letters showed that he was even more agitated over O'Neill's well-publicized marriage.

Because of Salinger's writing fame, he was chosen for a job in public relations at yet another base—Patterson Field in Fairfield, Ohio. As *New Yorker* editor, William Maxwell, later reported, Salinger "wrote publicity releases for Air Service Command in Dayton, Ohio, and used his three-day passes to go to a hotel and write stories."

Salinger continued fretting over the fact that he hadn't been chosen for Officer Candidate School. However, he was selected for service in the Counter Intelligence Corps. The CIC, a fairly recent invention of the military, was undergoing distinct changes as men were being trained for overseas duties. Late in 1943 and early in 1944, more than 800 servicemen were dispatched to England to be trained. This change meant yet another transfer, this time to Fort Holabird in Maryland for Salinger's initial training. The knowledge that he might leave for war and never return drove Salinger to write with more determination than ever. Early in 1944, the *Saturday Evening Post* purchased three of his stories at a price of $2,000 each. This sale netted a good profit for a regular Army boy and surely bolstered the ego of this beginning writer. The three stories, "Soft-Boiled Sergeant," "The Last Day of the Last Furlough," and "Both Parties Concerned," all dealt with war and the military. When the first two stories came out, J.D. was angry because the titles had been changed. He immediately became distrustful of editors and vowed that he would never let such a thing happen again.

Having made his way to England for his final training, Salinger awaited further orders and continued his writing. He was working on a novel starring the character Holden Caulfield, but he informed Whit Burnett that he did not want to be hurried. In the meantime, Burnett suggested that they create a book using some of Salinger's short stories. Burnett further suggested that the book be titled *The Young Folks*. Salinger cautiously provided Burnett with a list of eight stories that he felt might work as a book. He held back all stories about Holden Caulfield because the character and the subject matter would be used in his novel.

By late 1944, in a V-mail to Elizabeth Murray, Salinger described his depression and discouragement and his readiness to come home. The brutal, savage fighting slowly took its toll on his mind and spirit. The light breezy tone of patriotism was gone, replaced by a tone of despair. In the story, "A

Boy in France," the character, Babe, is in his foxhole reading a letter from his younger sister, Mattie; the letter closes with her telling him, "Please come home soon." After reading the words, he repeats them again and again like a desperate, despondent cry.

In the spring of 1945, Germany surrendered, ending the war in Europe. By summer, Salinger found that he was having great difficulty coping with reality from one day to the next. In July, he voluntarily sought help at an Army hospital in Nuremberg. In a letter to Hemingway from his hospital bed, Salinger admitted his concern about the possibility of receiving a discharge for psychiatric reasons. He thought it could have a negative effect on his writing career. But his fears were unfounded, as he received a general discharge.

Salinger stayed on in Europe doing civilian work with the Department of Defense while he continued to recuperate. He met and married a young woman named Sylvia and lived in a small town in Germany. Some biographers think that Sylvia was French, but Salinger's daughter Peggy confirms that she was German. Sylvia was actually an official in the Nazi party who had been arrested by Salinger. Peggy's Aunt Doris said the woman was "*very* German" and that their mother did not like her. Back in the states, the newlywed couple moved in with Salinger's parents, but Sylvia was ready to return to Europe within a few months. When she got back to Europe, she divorced him. Their marriage had lasted only eight months.

Now began a series of stories starring Salinger's familiar characters—Babe Gladwaller, his sister Mattie, and Vincent, Holden, and Kenneth Caulfield. These stories, which appear to be autobiographical, dealt with the aftereffects of surviving a terrible war, and the lives of war-ravaged soldiers suspended between the world of combat and the world of civilian readjustment.

Once again Salinger wound up living with his parents, but much had changed. He was no longer the same person. He spent nights with friends in Greenwich Village, where he played poker, hung out at his favorite bars, and ate at his favorite restaurants. One of his friends during this time, A.E. Hotchner, was a fellow writer. The two discussed their works with one another. Hotchner later expressed his amazement at Salinger's "complete confidence in his destiny as a writer—a writer he was and a writer he would always be, and what's more, an important writer."

In November 1946, after long years of waiting, the *New Yorker* informed Salinger that they planned to publish the story they had purchased from him before the war. The story appeared in the December 21 issue. The story was short—barely four magazine pages long—but it marked a momentous event in J.D.'s life. At last he felt he'd arrived as a writer. This first appearance in the famed magazine marked the beginning of a long and rather amazing working relationship.

THE CATCHER IN THE RYE

Whit Burnett continued discussions about publishing an anthology of J.D.'s short stories. The publisher would be Story Press's Lippincott imprint. The stories were selected, authors were chosen to provide endorsements, and a small advance check was submitted to Salinger. The plan was to bring out the book of short stories to establish Salinger's name, followed by his novel, which was one-third completed.

Burnett submitted the book of short stories to Lippincott, and they rejected it. Because Lippincott had the final say and Burnett could do nothing without them, all he could do was accept their judgment. Being as diplomatic as possible, Whit set up a meeting with Salinger at the Vanderbilt Hotel and attempted to explain what had transpired. Salinger grew sullen and angry, blaming his friend and mentor for the snafu. Already suspicious of the control editors exerted over writers, Salinger now applied this set of circumstances to all other editors. Never would he trust them again—that included Whit Burnett, the man who gave him his start.

The years between 1945 and 1947 were quiet ones for Salinger. In May 1947, one story appeared in *Mademoiselle* magazine entitled "A Young Girl in 1941 with No Waist at All," loosely based on his time spent as entertainment director on the *MS Kungholm*. In a note to the magazine, he let it be known that he did not believe in contributors' columns. The brief author's biography that accompanied most short stories stated this, and further noted, "He did say, however, that he started to write at eight and never stopped, that he was with the Fourth Division and that he almost always writes of very young people—as in his story [on] page 222."

The girl in "A Young Girl" is described as "just past the last minutes of her girlhood." This becomes an especially telling and poignant phrase, as shown in Salinger's future writings and in his life as a whole—he continually lived out his fascination with girls of this age.

Earlier in the year, Salinger finally got a small apartment of his own in Tarrytown in Westchester County, New York. The middle-class community was quite a contrast to his room in his parents' Park Avenue apartment. Although he wrote constantly, few stories were published at this time.

Being off and away must have proved agreeable, because the next move took Salinger even farther from home. After settling in a barn studio in

Stamford, Connecticut, Salinger wrote his most distinctive story to date, "A Perfect Day for Bananafish." Accepted by the *New Yorker*, the story appeared in the issue dated January 31, 1948. The story involves a young man so emotionally damaged by the war that he cannot connect with reality. At the end of the story, the young man commits suicide.

By now Salinger had received what was known as a "first-rejection contract" with the *New Yorker*. This meant they had the right to review his new stories first, before he submitted them elsewhere. For this privilege, they paid him an annual retainer. His association with the *New Yorker* gave Salinger the notoriety he longed for, in addition to respect from editors. Here, he could count on being contacted for approval on every detail, including the story title. Things were looking better.

Another postwar story appeared in *Good Housekeeping* in February 1948. The story, similar to Salinger's experience in Europe prior to the war, was about a young man in Vienna who finds out that the girl he met and fell in love with was exterminated in a Nazi concentration camp. It proves reminiscent of the family that Salinger lived with and came to love during his visit to Vienna.

In 1949, Salinger received a letter through the *New Yorker* from an editor at Harcourt Brace stating that they were interested in publishing a book of his short stories. He did not answer them for a month, showing the ambivalence he had developed toward editors, and instead showed up unannounced at the publisher's New York offices. There, Salinger told editor Robert Giroux that he wanted to publish his novel first. They shook hands and sealed the deal for the upcoming novel. Giroux described Salinger as a "tall sad-looking young man with a long face and deep-set black eyes. . . ."

Back in Westport, Salinger was constantly at work on his novel. Friends he met at the time knew all about the book, but naturally had no idea that it would become a famous classic novel.

When Salinger's short story, "Uncle Wiggily in Connecticut," appeared in the *New Yorker* magazine, Samuel Goldwyn purchased film rights. This was a first for Salinger—something he'd dreamed about since his college days. The movie starred Susan Hayward and Dana Andrews and took most of 1949 to produce. It opened early in 1950. During production, Salinger had no input whatsoever and, as a result, the plot had little to do with the original story. Victor Young wrote the theme song, "My Foolish Heart," which became a nightclub favorite and won an Oscar. Susan Hayward was also nominated for an Oscar for playing the female lead. Reviews of the movie were caustic, especially the one in the *New Yorker* written by John McCarten. He pointed out that the picture was so "full of soap-opera clichés," it was "hard to believe that it was wrung out of a short story . . . that appeared in this austere magazine a couple of years ago."

No matter how much the press disdained it, Salinger disdained it more. His dream of going to Hollywood turned into a nightmare, causing him to turn his back on movies completely. In future years, studios begged to purchase the rights to *The Catcher in the Rye*, but were repeatedly turned down. Perhaps it is for this reason that the character Holden Caulfield exhibits such rage against the movies, as Salinger was about halfway finished writing the novel when the movie, *My Foolish Heart*, opened in New York City.

While his treatment of the subject of education in his stories may reflect Salinger's uneasiness about having never received his degree, in 1949, he accepted an invitation to speak at Sarah Lawrence College, an all-girls school north of Manhattan. Standing before a group of intelligent and attractive young girls and answering their many questions made him terribly ill at ease. He later commented that instead of speaking to them, he should have shouted out the names of all his favorite writers—all of whom were dead. But he didn't. He struggled through to the end and knew when he left that he would never speak before a group again.

Five years after the war, Salinger wrote yet another story about the emotional damage suffered by those in combat. With the publication of "For Esmé—With Love and Squalor," which appeared in the *New Yorker* in April 1950, Salinger received more mail from his readers than for any story so far. The name of J.D. Salinger was definitely becoming well known in America, especially among readers of the *New Yorker*.

In August, the Esmé story appeared in *World Review* in London, where publisher Hamish Hamilton saw it. He immediately sent a telegram to Salinger in care of the *New Yorker*, saying that he wanted to publish whatever J.D. produced in the future. In subsequent correspondences, Salinger explained to Hamilton about his novel in progress. Hamilton responded by saying that he was willing to publish at Salinger's convenience.

In the fall of 1950, J.D. met a young schoolgirl named Claire Douglas at a party in New York. The 16-year-old Claire had just begun her senior year at Shipley, a girl's boarding school in Bryn Mawr, Pennsylvania. Claire was movie-star beautiful. She had worked that summer as a model for designer Nan Duskin and was wearing a blue linen dress that the designer allowed her to wear for the season. Both Claire and J.D. arrived at the party with dates, which kept their conversation to a minimum. Claire, however, was in awe of Salinger. The next day, Salinger called the hostess and was able to get Claire's address at Shipley. The two began corresponding sporadically during Claire's senior year.

Only a couple of months after meeting Claire, Salinger submitted a finished version of *The Catcher in the Rye* to Giroux at Harcourt Brace. The moment he read the book, Giroux felt lucky to be its editor. However, when he sent it to his boss, Eugene Reynal, Reynal nixed the whole deal by saying, "Is Holden Caulfield supposed to be crazy?" Realizing that Reynal did not understand the plot, Salinger asked to get his manuscript back. He then turned to the Boston firm of Little, Brown, who snapped up American rights. Shortly thereafter, Salinger's agent sold the novel to Hamish Hamilton in England.

The novel was also submitted to the *New Yorker* in hopes that it might publish excerpts. In a surprise move, the magazine rejected the idea. Several of the editors read it and did not care for the novel at all. Their main reason for the rejection, however, lay in the fact that they published writers not because they were novelists, but because they were writers for the *New Yorker*—attention stayed focused on the magazine and only the magazine. Salinger was furious at this decision.

The people at Little, Brown soon found out what a challenge they had on their hands with Salinger. He insisted that there be no advance galleys and no review copies sent to the press. There would be no publicity of any sort, and he demanded that his photo not appear on the back cover. His demands came too late, and many of the galleys had already been shipped. He chose not to submit to any interviews except one, the *Book-of-the-Month Club News*.

In a rare move, the Book-of-the-Month Club—which seldom, if ever, featured first novels—had chosen *Catcher* for its midsummer list. As part of the arrangement, Salinger agreed to give an interview. His agreement came in part because William Maxwell of the *New Yorker* conducted the interview. In the interview, Salinger seems to speak more as writer to writer than writer to reader as he comments:

> I think writing is a hard life. But it's brought me enough happiness that I don't think I'd ever deliberately dissuade anybody (if he had talent) from taking it up. The compensations are few, but when they come, if they come, they're very beautiful.

In the same publication, Clifton Fadiman, a board member of the Book-of-the-Month Club gushed over the book. "Read five pages and you are inside Holden's mind, almost as incapable of escaping from it as Holden is himself. That rare miracle of fiction has again come to pass: a human being has been created out of ink, paper, and the imagination."

When *Catcher* hit the market in July, reviews were decidedly mixed but leaned toward favorable. Some reviewers warned that the book was "not fit for children to read." In spite of the mixed reviews, the book made the *New York Times* best-seller list within two weeks. It stayed there for thirty weeks, climbing as high as number four.

Almost immediately, Salinger grew nervous about the hubbub created by the book. When Little, Brown released the third printing, the photo on the back cover was missing. None of the fame brought joy to J.D. Salinger. He told a friend that he did enjoy a small part of it, but most of the fame was "hectic and progressively and personally demoralizing."

Before the book was released, Hamish Hamilton came to the States and met with Salinger and the two of them seemed to hit it off. Salinger trusted Hamilton as much as he trusted any editor. In mid-May, Salinger then planned a trip to England to work with Hamilton on the British version of *Catcher* and to avoid publicity in the States when the book came out in July. Before he left, he went to see Claire Douglas who was back home in New York after graduating from Shipley. Coincidentally, she was also leaving the country. Her aged father, Robert Langdon Douglas (who was already 70 when she was born) was dying in Italy.

When Salinger arrived in England, Hamish Hamilton and his wife, Yvonne, saw to it that he was entertained properly. They took him to see Laurence Olivier and Vivien Leigh starring in the stage production of *Antony and Cleopatra*. After the show, they all went to dinner together because "Larry and Vivien" were personal friends of the Hamiltons.

While in England, Salinger visited the literary tourist spots: Shakespeare country, Wordsworth country, Brontë country, and Austen country. He especially loved Scotland and the moors of West Riding in Northern England. Salinger timed his trip to England just before *Catcher* hit the bookstores in August.

When he returned from England, Salinger didn't go to his country home, but instead took an apartment on East 57th Street. Perhaps he felt he would be more obscure in the city than in the country. In spite of the fact that he asked to receive no reviews, he not only received them, but went over them carefully. After the first flurry of praise had died down, magazines such as *Catholic World* were hard on the book for excessive swearing and coarse language.

When the British reviews came in, they were mostly negative and book sales were much slower than in the United States. The *Times Literary Supplement* wrote:

> Mr. Salinger . . . has not achieved sufficient variety in this book for a full-length novel. The boy is really very touching; but the endless stream of blasphemy and obscenity in which he thinks, credible as it is, palls after the first chapter. One would like to hear more of what his parents and teachers have to say about him.

Despite the negative British reviews, Salinger went right back to work. His newest story, a long and unusual piece entitled, "De Daumier-Smith's Blue Period," was submitted to the *New Yorker*. It was at this time that *New Yorker's* founding editor, Harold Ross, was extremely ill with cancer. Salinger held Ross in utmost respect, but most of his dealings were with Gus Lobrano. When Lobrano informed Salinger that the magazine had rejected "De Daumier-Smith's Blue Period," Salinger was extremely upset. He wrote back and said that he was profoundly disheartened by the rejection.

When Ross died in November, Salinger attended the services along with the rest of the *New Yorker* family. Ross's replacement, William Shawn, had been with the magazine since the late 1930s. In Shawn, Salinger found the kindly older-brother type of editor that he felt he needed. Twelve years Salinger's senior, Shawn was not the Ivy League type that proved repulsive to Salinger. Shawn was known for being courteous, considerate, and loyal. To his credit, Salinger set aside "De Daumier-Smith's Blue Period" and continued to work amicably with William Shawn.

AWAY FROM PUBLIC VIEW

Salinger invited his sister Doris to take a holiday with him to New England in the fall of 1952. Doris was a divorcee working as a buyer for the Green Room at Bloomingdale's. J.D.'s ulterior motive for the trip was to look for a house that would enable him to live in seclusion and concentrate solely on his writing.

When they stopped for lunch in Windsor, Vermont, they began talking with a local real estate agent. After lunch, the agent drove them over the covered bridge that separated Windsor from Cornish, New Hampshire, and up into the steep hills to show them a 90-acre piece of property and a ramshackle house. Doris later told her niece, "It wasn't a house, Peggy, it was a disaster!" The place had no heat and no running water. It may not have looked like much, but it fit perfectly with the description found in *Catcher*:

> . . . I'd build me a little cabin somewhere with the dough I made and live there for the rest of my life. I'd build it right near the woods, but not right in them, because I'd want it to be sunny as hell all the time . . . I'd meet this beautiful girl that was also a deaf-mute and we'd get married . . . If we had any children, we'd hide them somewhere. We could buy them a lot of books and teach them how to read and write by ourselves.

Salinger purchased the property and spent the first winter cutting wood with his new chain saw and carrying buckets of water. He had no phone, and often had to rely on his neighbors—an artist and his wife—at the foot of the hill for messages. When Salinger received a call from his agent or an editor, the artist would drive up the hill to summon him. While Salinger seemed to have achieved the remoteness he yearned for, he was probably summoned regularly during his work with Little, Brown in publishing his book of short stories. *Nine Stories* appeared in the United States in April 1953 and in England two months later. Timed to correspond with the release of *Catcher* in paperback, the book was deemed a commercial success. It stayed on the *New York Times* best-seller list for three months, an almost unheard-of feat for a book of short stories. As before, Salinger insisted that he didn't want to receive any reviews. Reading reviews, he said, was only a distraction to his current work.

When he first moved to Cornish, Salinger wasn't much of a recluse. He showed up at cocktail parties in town with some of the local teachers, writers, and retired military officers. He even invited them to his house from time to time. He also struck up a friendship with several of the town's teenagers, went to their ballgames, and hung out with them at an eating place called Harrington's Spa. For the out-of-town games, he let them pile into his Jeep and filled in as their chauffeur.

One student, Shirlie Blaney, recalled that when the kids first told her they were going up to his house, she was hesitant. Shirlie, more than the others, realized what a famous author he was and did not want to impose. When she decided to go along, she was surprised at Salinger's reaction, "He seemed to be delighted. He cried, 'Come on in' and started bringing out the Cokes and potato chips." He brought out records and played the hi-fi and acted as though he didn't want them to leave. After that he was like one of the gang.

In the fall of 1953, Shirlie and her friends were writing their monthly school page for the Windsor *Daily Eagle*. Because there wasn't much news in the town, Shirlie had the idea of interviewing Salinger, whom all the kids called Jerry. To her surprise, he agreed. Over lunch and Cokes at Harrington's Spa, they made history—it was one of the few interviews J.D. Salinger ever gave.

To Shirlie's great surprise, the paper did not publish the article on their school page, but instead displayed it prominently on the editorial page of the *Daily Eagle*. After that, when the teens went to see Salinger, it seemed that no one was home. Eventually, a fence with a locked gate barred the way. Whether he was upset with the teens, or back into his writing, no one could tell. However, in past relationships, Salinger was coldly unforgiving when he felt he'd been wronged.

Salinger was still interested in the young schoolgirl named Claire, who was now studying at Radcliffe. She began to spend time with Salinger at his home in Cornish and very soon found herself totally wrapped up in his life. The two of them contrived a person named "Mrs. Trowbridge" who supposedly acted as Claire's chaperone for weekends away from college. Together they wrote humorous letters signed by Mrs. Trowbridge and mailed them to Claire's mother. Claire was a very young-looking 19; Salinger was 34.

Claire would later tell her daughter, "The whole world was your father—everything he said, wrote, and thought. I read the things he told me to read, not the college stuff nearly as much, looked on the world through his eyes, lived my life as if he were watching me." Eventually, Salinger pressured Claire to drop out of school and come away to live with him in Cornish. When she refused, he dropped out of sight. Claire, who had survived a terrible childhood, was devastated. Unable to handle the fears of rejection and abandonment, she quickly married a boy from school and was horribly unhappy. The marriage was annulled within the year.

Even before the terrors of WWII encroached upon Claire Douglas's childhood in England, she could remember no happiness. Her mother was the third wife of Robert Langdon Douglas, a man many years her senior. Douglas at one time was an Anglican priest with a parish in Oxford who later became an art dealer and historian. Claire was the last of "fifteen or so children," according to Peggy Salinger.

Claire told Peggy stories of growing up with unkind and insensitive governesses. During the London Blitz, thousands of children were removed from the city for their own safety. Instead of sending their children to relatives in the country, as many families did, the Douglases sent Claire to a strict convent boarding school. She was only five years old. Her elder brother Gavin was with her, but he gave her no comfort. She described Gavin as a boy who liked to cause pain.

Two years later, the children were informed that their home in London had been bombed and burned to the ground. Claire's cat, Tiger Lily, was never found. Fortunately, the Douglases were out for the evening and their lives were spared.

For further safety, Claire and Gavin were put on a ship with other British children and sent to America, where they would live with foster families. On the way, a sister ship—also carrying hundreds of children—was hit by a German torpedo and burst into flames. Claire watched as the ship sank and all the children died.

Claire's parents came to America shortly after Claire arrived, but they did not ask her to come live with them. Between foster homes and boarding school, Claire knew little or nothing of a loving home and family. It was disastrous for the fragile young Claire Douglas to become associated with an author who loved his writing above all else—especially an author who insisted upon total isolation.

When Claire was released from her first marriage, Salinger reappeared. She was only four months away from her graduation day at Radcliffe, when he again presented her with the same choice: him or her degree. She immediately dropped out of school. They were married in Bradford, Vermont, by a justice of the peace on February 17, 1955. Salinger later told Peggy that he never forgave his two friends—witnesses at the wedding—for not warning him about the obvious mistake he was making.

The couple settled down in the house tucked away in the hills near Cornish. J.D. started building a bunker-type studio where he could work without distractions. The structure was made of cinder blocks and was painted dark green with a translucent green plastic roof. It had an overhang on one side to protect the stacks of wood that he had cut for winter. An old-fashioned wood-burning stove heated the one-room studio. There Salinger spent long hours at his work, sometimes failing to return to the house at all, sleeping on the cot that was shoved up against one wall.

Salinger got interested in Eastern religions after the war, but never seemed to fully connect or stay with any of them. Each time he turned to a new philosophy, he forced Claire to study it, too. His interests eventually included Zen Buddhism, Vedanta Hinduism, Kriya yoga, Christian Science, Scientology, the works of Edgar Cayce, homeopathy and acupuncture, and macrobiotics. A story entitled "Teddy," featured in the *New Yorker* in 1953, was one of the first stories that openly reflected his attachment to Eastern religions.

In December 1955, Margaret Ann (nicknamed Peggy) was born into this precarious family situation. Being a new mother, having no family skills, and being virtually alone in the middle of the wilderness with no phone proved to be a nightmare for Claire. She later confided to her daughter that on a trip to New York when Peggy was 18 months old, Claire devised a plan of escape. She managed to slip away from Salinger and stayed with her mother and stepfather while she received psychiatric treatment. The plan almost worked.

After four months, J.D. showed up begging Claire to return to Cornish. She did. But she never stopped wondering how different her life would have been if she hadn't caved in to his demands. Claire became strong enough to insist that she and her daughter should be allowed to have friends. She also asked her husband to build a proper nursery and to have a nice lawn with play equipment. She added that she wanted permission for Peggy to have access to a *regular* doctor. J.D. agreed.

Meanwhile Salinger's writing continued in the green studio. "Franny" had appeared in the *New Yorker* in January 1955, followed by "Zooey," in 1957. Franny and Zooey are both members of Salinger's fictional Glass family made famous throughout his years of writing.

In February 1960, the Salinger family was rounded out with the birth of his son, Matthew.

THE "CATCHER CULT"

All the children in Salinger's writings are precocious and full of extraordinary wisdom. Adult characters eagerly sought for and valued their input and opinions. As she grew up in the Salinger household, Peggy Salinger found it increasingly difficult to compete with her father's fictional characters, who behaved so perfectly.

When Peggy and Matthew were little, there were very few visitors in their home. An older lady named Mrs. Cox came to the house uninvited when she heard that a young mother lived there with a baby and no help. Her forthrightness and strong Yankee demeanor blustered right past the restrictions Salinger had instituted.

Another guest, a friend of Salinger from before his marriage to Claire, was the respected Judge Learned Hand and his wife. The Hands spent their summers in Cornish and kept up with the area news by corresponding with Salinger throughout the winter months. Peggy remembered the judge as a kind man who listened to her and conversed with her when she was a preschooler. Letters written to the judge show that Salinger gave the man fatherly respect, when true respect was something Salinger rarely gave to anyone.

Salinger's letters during 1955 refer to his diligent work on the story "Raise High the Roof Beam, Carpenters." The long manuscript required a great deal of editing to cut it back to the length required by the *New Yorker*. By now, Salinger and *New Yorker* editor William Shawn had developed an excellent working relationship and became close friends.

Shawn's secretary, Mary Kierstead, described Shawn as a wonderful man. "Writers thought it was a privilege to have him as an editor," she said. "He could change a sentence with a comma or with one word. He was always on the writer's side . . . . When Salinger came to New York, they worked in Mr. Shawn's office at his desk, which was a big table. They were always very amicable with one another." Eventually, Salinger's stories were no longer shown around the offices of the *New Yorker*, but went straight to Shawn. Salinger was only one of two authors whose work Shawn personally edited line by line.

Salinger continued to write satire about Ivy League intellectuals; at the same time the same people began writing reams of copy about Salinger. Literary magazines and academic journals featured countless critical essays about Salinger's fiction, taking it apart and examining it closely. The more Salinger attempted to fade from sight, the more prominent he became.

When *Cosmopolitan* magazine celebrated its 25th anniversary in 1956, they chose to feature Salinger's work in their Diamond Jubilee Issue. The magazine owned the rights to "The Inverted Forest" and therefore could run it with or without Salinger's permission. They ran the story using the name SALINGER in large block letters as an eye-catching headline.

A kind of "Catcher cult" arose during the teen revolution of the mid-1950s. Movies such as *The Wild One* and *Rebel Without a Cause* catered to dissatisfied youth, helping to give voice to their feelings of frustration. Many of them identified deeply with Holden Caulfield. In most high schools the book was required reading. This meant that thousands of teens who might not otherwise have read the book were introduced to *Catcher*. Another consistent theme that hit home with adolescents was Salinger's aversion to formal education.

During the winter of 1956–1957, Salinger worked feverishly on "Zooey," and even canceled plans to take his family to Europe for the summer. In letters to Judge and Mrs. Hand, he expressed his amazement over Claire's tolerance of the harsh winters and constant isolation. He seemed oblivious to the fact that his wife was near the breaking point.

When "Zooey" came out in May 1957, Signet, the company that published *Catcher* and *Nine Stories* in paperback, ran a big ad in the *New York Times*. The ad connected the release of the paperback edition to the newly released story "Zooey," a much talked-about new piece of fiction. Salinger was furious. He shot off terse telegrams to Ned Brown of Little, Brown expressing his disgust at the marketing ploy.

Roger Machell, an associate of Hamish Hamilton, arrived in New York in February 1958. He notified Salinger but received a curt reply that the author was much too busy to come to New York to meet with him. The Britishman was not offended. He had long ago decided that Salinger was "perhaps the most brilliant but certainly by far the nuttiest author I've ever known." Machell went on to say, "His real mania is publishers. He realizes books must be published but wishes they didn't. . . . I would say he has a profound hatred of all publishers."

Salinger eventually came to the conclusion that his work did not need to be published at all. He continued to write without submitting his work to publishers. In the interim, incidents continued to occur which, in his mind, justified this course of action.

One such incident involved his British publishers. In 1953, Hamish Hamilton had purchased *Nine Stories* and retitled it *For Esmé—With Love and Squalor*. It did not sell well, but when there was new interest in Salinger in the late 1950s, Hamilton decided to sell the paperback rights to Ace Books, a new division of Harborough Publishing. In retrospect, Hamilton probably made an unwise decision, because Ace aimed toward the mass market without concern for literary style. Perhaps Hamilton grew impatient because Salinger's books had not made much profit in England. Whatever the case, Ace published the paperback with a cheap, appallingly illustrated cover. The cover blurb totally detracted from the quality of the book: "Explosive and Absorbing—A Painful and Pitiable Gallery of Men, Women, Adolescents, and Children." It gave no hint that the book contained a collection of short stories.

Nothing was said to Salinger, but he eventually found out about it when a Hamilton staff member accidentally mentioned it. In his anger, Salinger placed total blame on Hamilton, who had no control over the paperback cover.

> Jerry, not unnaturally, was furious and held me personally responsible. Nothing I could say could persuade him that the hardcover publishers had no influence over paperback jackets. I did everything in my power, including offering to go to America, but to no avail. . . . We had an option on his next novel, but Jerry said he would rather not be published in England than by me.

This was a costly error for Hamilton. J.D. Salinger never spoke to him again.

During 1958, Salinger worked on another very lengthy novella entitled, "Seymour: An Introduction." Illnesses and family distractions drove him to try working in the offices of the *New Yorker* to finish the work. A *New Yorker* college intern remembered meeting Salinger: "He'd come up to the office at night, and there'd be just the two of us in this big dark building. He worked seven days a week and it was the hardest work I've ever seen anyone do. But he was never too busy to stop, light a cigarette, and have a cup of coffee and talk with me." One night he presented the young man with an autographed copy of *Catcher*. Salinger successfully completed "Seymour," and it appeared in the New Yorker June 6, 1959.

For reasons not fully understood, Salinger decided to emerge from seclusion by means of a letter to the editor of the *New York Post* regarding the unjust treatment of prisoners on death row. "Justice," he wrote, "is at best one of those words that makes us look away or turn up our coat collars, and justice—without mercy—must easily be the bleakest, coldest combination of words in the language."

The irony of such comments was the fact that—as Peggy Salinger later revealed in her biography—Claire had been relegated to a type of prison sentence just by becoming the wife of J.D. Salinger. And perhaps the green bunker on the hillside, initially designed for seclusion, was now becoming its own self-imposed prison.

Soon after the birth of son Matthew in 1960, several major magazines began a search for the true J.D. Salinger. The more he attempted to hide, the more challenge he presented for the brightest and best of newshounds.

The first who attempted to break through the fortress was Mel Elfin of *Newsweek*. Elfin's strategy was to comb the town of Cornish for anyone who might provide a few details. One of the people he spoke to was the artist neighbor, Bertrand Yeaton, whose telephone J.D. had used when he first arrived in the area. The neighbor told about Salinger's structured work habits, commenting that he "works like a dog." He went on to give a brief description of the inside of the small studio. "On the wall of the studio, Jerry has a series of cup hooks, to which he clips sheaves of notes. They must deal with various characters and situations, because when an idea occurs to him, he takes down the clip, makes the appropriate notation and places it back on the proper hook." The article appeared in the May 1960 issue of *Newsweek*. It featured only two photos—Salinger's mailbox and a shot of the house barely visible through a stand of trees. Edward Kosner of the *New York Post* made the next attempt. His article consisted mostly of the names of people who would *not* talk about Salinger. No new information was shared.

Meanwhile, Salinger had made the decision to combine two stories and publish a book entitled *Franny and Zooey*. The release date was to be early fall of 1961. At first, Salinger said he would write an introduction, but quickly changed his mind agreeing to write only a brief statement. He gave strict rules about the release: simple and plain cover design, no advance publicity, no advance sales to book clubs.

When the news broke that there would be another book by J.D. Salinger, the press once again took up their search. *Time* magazine assigned an entire team of reporters to search the countryside for every snippet of information. At one point they succeeded in finding Claire's brother, Gavin Douglas, whom they bailed out of a local drunk tank. He was the source of much of the basic information for *Time's* cover story dated September 15, 1961.

The last article in the series came from the celebrated *Life* magazine. They didn't do much better than the previous reporters. There was a photo of the mailbox, the Salingers' two vehicles parked in a clearing across the road from the house, a yearbook photo of Claire, two dated photos of J.D., and a half-page spread of the Salingers' fence with a dog peering from beneath. Writer, Ernest Havemann, however, did get as far as the front door and described Claire holding the baby, with little Peggy standing in the background looking "friendly and expectant."

When *Franny and Zooey* was published in 1961, with its dedication to William Shawn and one-year-old Matthew Salinger, the jacket copy referred to other stories waiting in the wings. The truth of the matter was that the *New Yorker* had no other stories written by Salinger. The book hit the *New York Times* best-seller list and stayed there for six months, at one point reaching the number one spot. The public clamored for the book, but literary critics weren't as kind. Most were extremely negative. Some of them felt that the high sales volume was fueled by a morbid curiosity to see what Salinger was up to after all those years.

Hamish Hamilton soon found out that when a relationship with Salinger was over, it was truly over. Salinger refused Hamilton's advance of £10,000 for the rights to *Franny and Zooey*. He then turned around and sold it to another company for £4,000, but the book sold poorly in England anyway.

Evidently, the financial success of *Franny and Zooey* compelled Salinger to repeat the process. This time he put together "Seymour: An Introduction" and "Raise High the Roof Beam, Carpenters." The book, released January 1963, brought the worst reviews to date. In the jacket copy he mentioned having "several new Glass stories coming along—waxing, dilating—each in its own way, but I suspect the less said about them, in mixed company, the better." The comments were vague and misleading. There may have been more Glass stories, but none ever appeared in print. Following this book, one more Salinger story appeared in the *New Yorker*—then nothing.

In the spring of 1963, President John F. Kennedy invited the Salingers to a reception honoring American writers at the White House. The reclusive Salinger refused the invitation, even after Jackie Kennedy called and spoke to both J.D. and Claire. Claire later commented, "Jerry didn't want me to feel I was worth anything, and above all, he wanted to make sure that I be prevented from having a chance to fall into the feminine vice of vanity. . . ." In the poignant sadness of the moment, Claire penned a haiku:

> *Having to decline*
> *The White House invitation,*
> *She dreams of her gown.*

The next November, President Kennedy was shot and killed. Peggy Salinger recalled her father weeping as he watched the funeral on television. She said it was the only time she ever saw him cry in her whole life.

The year after Kennedy's death, Whit Burnett planned to publish an anthology of stories taken from past issues of his magazine. It was going to be called *Story Jubilee: 33 Years of Story*. Whit wanted to use one of J.D.'s early stories, but the request was denied. Salinger did, however, agree to write an introduction. When he was finished, Salinger turned the piece over to Burnett. The essay was not about the anthology, but about Salinger's association with him. Burnett was upset and had no choice but to turn it down, an act that further eroded their relationship.

By 1966, Claire could no longer endure her situation. The isolation, the absent husband and father, the strict demands of a spouse who wanted everything in the home to be perfect, were causing her serious physical and mental consequences. She sought the care of a physician in Claremont, New Hampshire, Dr. Gerard Gaudrault. He found that she was suffering from nervous tension, sleeplessness, and weight loss. Shortly thereafter, she filed for divorce.

The divorce was granted October 3, 1967. The cause was "treatment as seriously to injure health and endanger reason." Claire was awarded the house, the land, the children, and $8,000 per year in child support. The decree also stated that Salinger would be responsible for funding the children's education. He was permitted lenient visitation rights.
Salinger moved to nearby acreage that he had purchased several years earlier. He subsequently built a new house on the property. At this point, his seclusion could not have been more complete.

For years after divorcing, Claire struggled with a number of fleeting relationships with much younger men. Finally, she returned to college and got her bachelor's degree in 1969. She went on to earn a master's degree in education, another master's degree in social work, and eventually earned her doctorate in psychology from the Saybrook Institute of San Francisco in 1984. She had a private practice in New York City. Later, she moved to California to be near her son, Matthew, and to set up a child psychology practice in Malibu.

THE SEARCH FOR SALINGER

As Peggy Salinger was growing up, she found it increasingly difficult to be the "swell" little trooper that her father expected her to be. "My mind didn't bend," she said, "it split in such a way that I became almost two people: the part of me that played with my friends and thought my own secret thoughts and the part of me that was his voice in my head and enabled me to be a person he loved."

The fear of rejection constantly hung over Peggy's head because she'd seen how her father snapped off relationships almost at will when he was offended. On one occasion when father and daughter had a disagreement, J.D. talked to her about the problem in an adult manner, warning her that they'd better find a way to make up quickly because "when I'm through with a person, I'm *through* with them." Then he added, "I'll always love you, but when I lose respect for a person, I'm done with them. Finished." These words made Peggy's stomach churn. A man who wrote that there is no difference in age between 10 and 80 would have little understanding about the reality of what was and was not age-appropriate for his own daughter.

In *Franny and Zooey*, Zooey tells his sister, Franny, "And don't tell me again that you were ten years old. Your age had nothing to do with what I'm talking about. There are no big *changes* between ten and twenty—or ten and eighty for that matter." Such thinking made growing up as the daughter of J.D. Salinger extremely difficult.

Whit Burnett, more than most people, knew what it meant to be cut off from Salinger's friendship. In 1968, he once more asked J.D. for a story to be included in an upcoming anthology entitled, *This Is My Best*. This book was in no way connected to *Story* magazine. Once again, Salinger refused, reminding his one-time mentor that they'd been over this subject many times in the past.

That same year J.D. took Peggy and Matthew on a vacation to England. Peggy's highest hope was that she might meet Paul McCartney of the Beatles. In the midst of all the sightseeing and meeting of some of J.D.'s old friends, he kept a rendezvous with a young girl with whom he'd been corresponding. The letters had evidently blossomed into a relationship. However, when J.D. met her face-to-face and saw that she was not attractive, the relationship was over. And Peggy never got to meet Paul McCartney.

By 1970, Salinger had made up his mind never to be published again. With *Catcher* continuing to sell at a steady pace, he was never in dire financial straits. It allowed him to turn his back on the publishing world altogether. In a move almost unheard of in the publishing industry, he repaid a $75,000 advance to Little, Brown for an upcoming work of fiction.

In 1972, a cover article in the *New York Times* captured Salinger's attention. Joyce Maynard, a freshman at Yale University—one of the first women to attend—had written an article entitled "An Eighteen-Year-Old Looks Back on Life." Her photo graced the cover. Salinger promptly went to his typewriter and wrote Joyce a one-page letter in which he warned her against the dangers of the "establishment."

Maynard was not the type of girl who needed such a warning. She'd been making her own way for quite some time. The daughter of an artist father and writer mother, Maynard had already been published in *Seventeen* and *Mademoiselle* before the attention-grabbing cover story for the *Times*. She'd lived through a troubled childhood and suffered from severe eating disorders. When she received Salinger's letter, which she called profound and insightful, she was deeply touched. She wrote back and they soon developed an ongoing correspondence.

Maynard's childhood home was in New Hampshire, so when she came home on a school break, she visited Salinger. Instead of returning to school where a full scholarship awaited her, she moved in with Salinger. Years later, a much wiser Joyce Maynard would write a book about this time in her life. Published in 1998, *At Home in the World* describes Salinger's controlling personality and how Joyce changed and adapted her life to please him.

Peggy Salinger remembered how strange she felt knowing that her 54-year-old father kept company with a girl two years older than her. "He may have mentioned her, but I don't remember anything but the strangeness of meeting Joyce Maynard. . . . I mean she was perfectly nice and everything, but who expects to find someone looking like a twelve-year-old girl?" Maynard, on the other hand, remembered Peggy Salinger as an honest, uncompromising, and self-possessed young lady of whom she was in awe.

Maynard remained with Salinger for nearly a year, during which time he took her to New York, bought her gifts, took her to lunch at the Algonquin Hotel, and introduced her to his friends, including William Shawn of the *New Yorker*. Among other problems in their relationship, they had a long-running disagreement about children. Maynard's heart was set on rearing a family, but Salinger was totally against the idea. During a Florida vacation, as they sat on the beach, Maynard again brought up the subject of children. Salinger told her to return to Cornish and pack her things and leave. That ended the relationship. It took Maynard many years to put her life together again.

As time passed, Salinger became more and more of an oddity and a legend. He was heard from only when he chose—most often when he was angry about having his privacy invaded. In 1977, a spoof indirectly involving Salinger surfaced when *Esquire* published a story with no byline, entitled "For Rupert—With No Promises." The style of the story, as well as the characters, had readers thinking that the author might be Salinger. It caused a big stir in the media, including a front page story in the *Wall Street Journal*. In actuality, the idea was cooked up by fiction editor Gordon Lish to bolster sales for the sinking magazine. Confessing that he'd had a bit too much to drink at the time, he sat down and wrote the story in one evening. Lish later capitalized on the idea and wrote other takeoffs on Salinger characters.

In 1974, a book entitled *The Complete Uncollected Short Stories of J.D. Salinger* was released by a young man named John Greenberg. The two volumes consisted of stories published between 1940 and 1948 in such magazines as *The Saturday Evening Post*, *Collier's*, and *Esquire*. Most importantly, they were printed without Salinger's permission. The books were peddled in person to bookstores at $1.50 each, and the stores were selling them at a hefty profit. Greenberg, who claimed to be from Berkeley, California, often varied in description from city to city. At one point he (or they) attempted to sell the book to Andreas Brown, manager of the Gotham Book Mart in New York City. Brown confronted the young man and asked him about the possibility of getting in trouble by publishing the stories without Salinger's permission. The man said he expected that he could always negotiate with Salinger's lawyers and promise to never do it again.

Brown refused to be involved and alerted Salinger about the matter. Within weeks, Salinger's lawyers filed a civil suit against John Greenberg and 17 bookstores in the New York area, alleging violation of the copyright laws. Even though the stories had appeared in periodicals, the copyrights were still in Salinger's name. The stores were prevented from selling any more unauthorized books and faced possible damage payments of thousands of dollars. Before the selling stopped, however, more than 25,000 copies had been sold at $3 to $5 each.

In the midst of the legal proceedings, Salinger broke his silence and placed a surprise phone call to express his anger at this invasion of privacy. Speaking to Lacey Fosburgh, a writer for the *New York Times* based in San Francisco, he explained that he never wanted those stories to be republished. "Some stories, my property, have been stolen," Salinger told Fosburgh. "Someone's appropriated them. It's an illicit act. It's unfair. Suppose you had a coat you liked and somebody went into your closet and stole it. That's how I feel." He further explained his personal sentiments about those particular stories. "I wrote them a long time ago and I never had any intention of publishing them. I wanted them to die a perfectly natural death." Then he added, "I'm not trying to hide the gaucheries of my youth. I just don't think they're worthy of publishing."

At the beginning of the call to Fosburgh, Salinger said that he would talk for only a minute, but the call lasted for nearly a half hour. He spoke about his present writing and his reluctance to publish. "There is a marvelous peace in not publishing," he said. "It's peaceful. Still. Publishing is a terrible invasion of my privacy. I like to write. I love to write. But I write just for myself and my own pleasure."

Being a good news reporter, Fosburgh asked the inevitable question, did he expect to publish another work soon? He said he didn't know just how soon. "I don't necessarily intend to publish posthumously," he said, "but I do like to write for myself." His parting words sounded somewhat pathetic: "I just want all this to stop. It's intrusive. I've survived a lot of things, and I'll probably survive this."

Fosburgh was amazed at her good fortune in having such a lengthy conversation with the reclusive Salinger. She wrote the article quoting Salinger word for word, and it wound up on the front page of the *New York Times*. As one thing led to another, the *Times* subsequently sent a reporter, Bill Roeder, to follow up and attempt a face-to-face interview with Salinger. Roeder, bolder than most, approached Salinger's front door and knocked. Salinger answered the door, and they engaged in a short awkward conversation. Roeder was unable to get any new information. The lawsuit that precipitated his phone call to the *New York Times* was finally settled in 1986 in Salinger's favor.

By 1976, the Salinger children were grown and on their own, although Peggy had been on her own much of the time even as an adolescent. Matthew seemed to be living out his father's dreams of becoming an actor. When he appeared in a production at Phillips Exeter School, Salinger emerged from seclusion to attend the play. A schoolmate of Matt's remembered being surprised at Salinger's gray hair and how very old he looked.

PRIVACY WARS

Early in the 1980s, London biographer Ian Hamilton (no relation to Hamish Hamilton) decided to attempt a full biography of J.D. Salinger. He began his project by writing to Salinger. He didn't expect to receive permission, and he didn't receive it. However, Hamilton was certain that he could procure enough material through legal means, and by using ethical journalism practices, to write a well-rounded biography.

Hamilton found that Salinger's friends and family were literally sworn to secrecy. However, through painstaking research he uncovered many sets of personal letters that gave a great deal of insight into the character and life of Salinger. By 1986, the book was finished and nearly ready for press. The book jacket was ready and the typesetting completed. The book was entitled *J.D. Salinger; A Writing Life*. Hamilton never thought of it as a true biography because he was so limited in the information he could use, but he did feel that it was the best anyone had ever done. He even secretly believed that Salinger would like the book. He was wrong.

In May 1986, Hamilton received a letter from Salinger's lawyers stating that he had read the bound galleys. He protested the use of unpublished letters, and unless they were removed, he would take legal action. Hamilton, at home in London at the time, rushed to New York and worked with Random House to decide how to cut back on the direct quotes. After weeks of work, a revision was sent to Salinger's lawyers. The Random House lawyers were confident that there would be no charges, because if there were, Salinger would have to appear in court—and they were certain that would never happen. They were wrong again.

Salinger claimed that the unpublished letters were worth a lot of money and that no one should be able to pick them up and use them. He was fully prepared to fight to the finish for his literary rights in order to protect his privacy. On October 10, 1986, 68-year-old J.D. Salinger traveled to New York to be interviewed for a court deposition. The deposition took six hours and was the first-ever extended interview of J.D. Salinger.

When the case went to court in November, the judge delivered a verdict in favor of permitting publication of the biography. The victory was celebrated not only by Hamilton, but by other writers and journalists all across the nation. The victory was short-lived. By December, Salinger had lodged his appeal, and Judges Jon O. Newman and Roger Miner reversed the first judgment. Publication of the biography was prohibited.

The final irony in Hamilton's mind was that Salinger got a lot more attention from the drawn-out lawsuit than he would have from the published biography. Salinger had been forced to copyright each personal letter, which means that for a fee of $10 anyone can visit the copyright office in Washington, D.C., and read them all. In addition, hundreds of newspaper and magazine articles had appeared since he filed the suit.

New York magazine stated, "In the course of this well-documented lawsuit, the public is learning more about Salinger than it has at any time during the last 34 years." Regarding the seriousness of the suit, the magazine went on to state, "And if the precedent-setting case is finally decided in favor of Salinger, the elusive author's influence on future biography, journalism and nonfiction could prove as indelible as his mark on modern fiction." Eventually, Hamilton went on to publish a book entitled, *In Search of J.D. Salinger*, which he referred to as his "legal version," containing no quotes from personal correspondence.

The events regarding Hamilton were strange, but there were even more strange happenings in the decade of the 1980s involving the name of J.D. Salinger. On December 8, 1980, a disturbed young man named Mark David Chapman approached Beatles singer, John Lennon, as he stepped from his limousine and shot him five times in the back. After the shooting, Chapman walked away, sat down on the curb, and began reading *The Catcher in the Rye*. Fascinated with the book and with the character of Holden Caulfield, 25-

year-old Chapman believed that the moment he killed Lennon, he would "become" Caulfield.

A man who loved children and saw adults as ugly and depressing, Chapman was a favorite counselor at YMCA camp. He felt it was his duty to save children from falling into the world of phony adults. So closely did he identify with Caulfield that while living in Hawaii, he asked to have his name changed to Holden Caulfield. When he failed to turn into Caulfield following the shooting, Chapman decided that the purpose of killing Lennon must have been to draw attention to the book. "Everybody's going to be reading this book—with the help of the god-almighty media," he told his lawyer. Chapman called himself "the catcher in the rye for this generation," believing that each generation must have its own catcher. While there was no death penalty in the state of New York at the time, many people believe if it had been in effect, Mark David Chapman would have been executed by now. Four months later, 26-year-old John Hinckley Jr. attempted to assassinate President Ronald Reagan. The president was shot, but not killed. Also wounded were James Brady, the president's press secretary, and Thomas Delahanty, a Washington, D.C. policeman. Secret Service agent, Timothy McCarthy, was also hit.

When investigators went through Hinckley's personal effects in a suitcase in his hotel room, they found a tattered copy of *The Catcher in the Rye*. In addition to the character Caulfield, Hinckley was also infatuated with film star Jodie Foster. He wrote her that he staged the assassination simply to impress her.

If two instances were not enough, a third tragedy occurred in July 1989. Actress Rebecca Schaeffer, star of a television sitcom, *My Sister Sam*, had been barraged with gifts and letters from a man named Robert John Bardo. The 21-year-old Bardo went to Schaeffer's apartment, and when she opened the door he shot and killed her. Police found the gun, a blood-soaked shirt, and a copy of *The Catcher in the Rye* in a neighborhood alley.

Despite the turmoil, the 1980s meant new relationships for Salinger. He became infatuated with Elaine Joyce, a star on the television sitcom *Mr. Merlin*. Initially, he approached her by letter—the same way he had approached Joyce Maynard. She answered his letter, and they corresponded for a while—she was in California and he was still in Cornish. Eventually, she came to New York and they spent time together. Breaking his seclusion, Salinger appeared at a dinner theater in Florida, where Joyce was featured in a play. Joyce was 36; Salinger was 62.

When that affair ended, he met a young woman from Cornish named Colleen O'Neill. They eventually married. Colleen was 50 years younger than Salinger.

In October 1992, there was a fire at the Salinger house in Cornish. It brought out fire trucks and emergency vehicles from a number of neighboring towns. The valiant efforts of firefighters saved about half the house and a new wing that was under construction. The public found out that there was a new Mrs. Salinger (Colleen O'Neill), because she identified herself when she called the fire department. The incident showed up in the media almost immediately; it was reported on CNN and in major newspapers.

In yet another flurry of news articles, there were reports that Salinger would again be published. The renewed interest began in 1997 with a small notice on *Amazon.com* naming *Hapworth 16, 1924* as an upcoming release. The publisher was listed as Orchises Press, a small obscure company in Alexandria, Virginia, run by a man named Roger Lathbury. *Hapworth* was the last story that appeared in the *New Yorker* under Salinger's byline. The news quickly spread. Suddenly, articles and reviews appeared in newspapers and magazines across the nation. One review, highly critical of the Hapworth story, was written by Michiko Kakutani, a book critic for the *New York Times*. After her negative review, the publication of the book was postponed.

Lathbury had agreed not to publicize the book, not to reveal any details about production such as print run, and not to give any details of his dealings with the author. He did say that buyers were waiting eagerly for the release of the book. At this writing, four years later, *Amazon.com* continues to promise that there *will* be a forthcoming book. The notice on the website reads as follows:

> As one might expect with a J.D. Salinger title, there are some twists and turns. The publisher of this title has asked us to pass along some information. First, the title has been delayed from its original March date. It's still coming out, but the exact publication date is not yet fixed. There can be unexpected delays in the publication process, especially with a title that is generating as much demand as this one, and unfortunately such delays are beyond our control. We always remain in frequent contact with our suppliers to make sure that we can get newly released books to you as quickly as possible.
>
> Orchises notes that all backorders will be honored and assures us the book is really being published. Second, the list price was raised in April from $15.95 to $22.25, and the discounts to distributors and booksellers is [sic] still somewhat confusing. Salinger has always refused to take the conventional route, and it looks like he's running true to form with the publication of this book.

Also on the Web page regarding *Hapworth 16, 1924*:

This item will be published in November 2002. You may order it now and we will ship it to you when it arrives.

Dragging out the publication date of a novella that needs no editing or revisions but only to be printed and bound appears to be another reminder to the public of how much J.D. Salinger wants to be forgotten and left alone.

EPILOGUE

Why has Salinger's reputation endured, why has the legend continued to grow, and why have his books continued to sell? Thousands of other works have come and gone since Salinger's books were published. Yet his one novel and three collections of 13 stories have remained steadily in print in many languages throughout the entire world. How can the voice of Holden Caulfield speak to the youth of succeeding generations?

People may try to answer these questions, but the phenomenon remains a mystery. Warren French, in *Salinger Revisited*, calls Salinger the man "who made a success of refusing to conform." Salinger turned his back on fame and fortune, preferring to remain private and aloof. Perhaps he stopped publishing because he could never stand criticism. (Even his own sister, Doris, believes that.) Or perhaps the whole thing has been one big publicity stunt.

In the more than 40 years since it was published, *The Catcher in the Rye* has sold more than 15 million copies in the United States alone. Salinger's other books sold millions of copies, too.

In 1999, Paul Alexander wrote a new biography of Salinger. For his research materials, Alexander, a one-time reporter for *Time* magazine, used newly opened archives and personal interviews with over 40 major literary figures. The book offers a fuller image of Salinger, but the mysteries remain unsolved.

In 2000, Margaret A. (Peggy) Salinger published her moving and revealing biography entitled *Dream Catcher*, featuring never-before-seen family photos of J.D. Salinger as a young father and family man. In her book, she courageously and honestly deals with her struggle of living under the control of a domineering and controlling, cult-like father and how it affected her life. Battling with eating disorders, phobias, suicidal tendencies, and a number of physical illnesses, she at last breaks out of bondage to find out who she truly is. Through the painful process, something had to give. "What began to crack," she wrote, "was my belief in the illusion of my father."

That fragile illusion may also have cracked for long-time fans and once-loyal readers. The dust jacket of Alexander's book says it more clearly:

> . . . the remarkable story of a man whose fictional creations became as real to him as friends, family, and lovers—a man who chose, in adolescence, to stop his life in a freeze frame and who had lingered in that fantasy world for a half century.

CLIFFORD MILLS

A Critical Perspective on the Writings of J.D. Salinger

More than almost any other writer, J.D. Salinger created his work and then left the stage; the characters that he brought to life, though, and one in particular, play on in a seemingly indefinite run. Teachers of English revere Salinger's most famous work, *The Catcher in the Rye*, to a degree approaching that of Twain's *Huckleberry Finn*; and Holden Caulfield, the protagonist of *Catcher*, continues to challenge his readers and to perform many roles at once: saint and cynic, insider and outsider, pacifist and rebel, nonconformist, masochist, optimist, liar, and learner of everything and nothing.

Salinger has been accused both of loving and of mocking his characters. While his biographers give some evidence that some of these "imaginary" figures were in fact all too real for him,[1] one can only imagine how Holden Caulfield, the Glass brothers and sisters, and the text's other characters stayed with Salinger and transformed his art. One can imagine Holden and Seymour Glass, especially, influencing and judging their creator in a perpetual dialogue—pulling him in very different directions even as they demand his protection.

The lure of a character is often determined by the writer's success in invoking an archetype. The writer doing the inventing—which is perhaps more akin to discovering—often appears torn between constructing a unified and clarified imaginative world for his or her characters to inhabit and damning them to a divided and chaotic one. Salinger, too, seems torn; in his work, one can see the dynamics among and within the characters, his methods of making these inventions look and feel like discoveries, and the kinds of worlds the characters live in.

THE CATCHER IN THE RYE (1951)

Readers often remember their first few minutes with the instantly familiar Holden Caulfield. This immediacy of rapport between the reader and Holden stems, in part, from the confessional nature of *The Catcher in the Rye*. The narrator makes known at the outset what he is *not* going to tell, trying to convince his audience that he's not going to follow their expectations or anyone else's. He declares his independence from his origins, and yet he confesses that he is worried about what his parents might think if he describes them. Thus at once he shows his possible estrangement from them *and* his hidden attachment to them. Holden says he is recalling what has happened; one learns later that he is now 17 years of age but was 16 during the December days he will recall. Whether this lapse of some six months has afforded him any more objectivity concerning his experiences is questionable.

Adding to this sense of familiarity, Holden's now famous style—slangy, nonliterary—adheres to the tradition of Huck Finn and other characters in early American "declamatory literature."[2] His speech is repetitious, filled with exaggerations and "realistic" expressions, including profanities. This works to lessen the distance between narrator and audience, fostering the illusion that one knows Holden personally. In expanding this knowing, one is allowed to see the inconsistencies among what Holden is thinking, what he is feeling, and what he is saying to others, culminating in an ability to intuit the disparity between what he is telling and what he is not.

Holden's narration of the story follows, more or less, the form of a pilgrimage, a journey in which the character enters, intentionally or accidentally, a previously unexperienced world, and then reenters his own world to find both it and himself profoundly altered. Holden's experiences at Pencey Prep (chapters 1–7) reflect the dichotomies inherent in his experience and environment. He recognizes the difference between the school's public image and its academic inefficacy. His favorite professor exhibits a gentleness compromised by snobbery, while Holden himself exhibits the snobbery of his own disdain for snobs. His roommate, Stradlater, demonstrates a cleanliness that merely masks his hidden filth. As Holden recognizes such dichotomies, he reacts with a "fight or flight" response to such people, institutions, and events—a primitive survivor's response to the world.

Chapters 8 through 20 describe Holden's nontriumphant return to his hometown, New York, and his manic-depressive attempts to lose and find himself in the city. These frantic and seemingly random wanderings enable him to see and experience people and places both familiar and unfamiliar. It is during these experiences that Holden tries on various masks, disguises, in an attempt to find himself. In one such instance he becomes the dorm janitor's son to a woman on the train to New York; another episode has him adopting the persona of "Jim Steele" (perhaps an early version of James Bond) to a prostitute and her pimp. These disguises are in effect disappearances, something Holden and, later, Franny Glass often fantasize about. Not only willing to try on certain new disguises, Holden is also able to recognize and to reject old disguises, disguises he no longer wants, such as his stories of going to Yale or Princeton or becoming an "organization man" in the city. He also tries to lose himself in the disguises of others—the Lunts, the Rockettes, the Christmas show, a movie, a progression of increasingly less real forms of entertainment. In his manic phase, Holden tries himself out at three bars (the hotel's Lavender Room, Ernie's in Greenwich Village, and the Wicker Bar on 54th)—each more attractive, but each more draining his manic and social impulses, than the one before as his physical setting becomes inversely proportional to his emotional state. However, none of these performances provides as much pleasure or relief as overhearing a child walking in the street singing, "If a body catch a body coming through the rye." Holden says the experience makes him "feel better" and "not so depressed any more." By the end of the second day in New York, however, he is exhausted, hung over, and collapsing, his mania gone and his depression a solid presence. He has devolved from a former combination playboy/hipster/20th-century aristocrat who used to summer in Maine and hits all the right clubs and bars, to a nearly homeless man out of touch with family, friends, and community. The insider has become an outsider; and why and how this inversion has taken place is one of the story's enduring questions.

Chapters 21 through 26 mark Holden's "recovery" and return and a renewal through reunions with (1) his sister, Phoebe, and her world of innocence, truth, and caring and (2) Mr. Antolini, the most helpful of his guides, who is "very nice." In the final chapter, Holden declares, "That's all I'm going to tell about." He has told more than one can make sense of with any single set of critical guidelines. As many critics have noted, very large questions are raised about what will happen to Holden next.[3] The desire to know more comes of the broad knowledge one has of him already.

The peripheral characters of *Catcher* are interspersed throughout the book, each having its own effect on Holden. Some, like D.B., Holden's brother and the first and last peripheral character invoked, exist only in Holden's memory but are no less powerful for it. D.B., a Hollywood scriptwriter who Holden admits comes to see him dutifully almost every weekend, affords Holden the opportunity to confide in his readers. Holden views D.B. as someone who has sold his soul as a "prostitute"; this is a judgment that Holden surely has withheld from his brother. He confides continually and seems to give to the reader a privileged access to his inner self an—illusion that critic Susan Mitchell explains in detail.[4]

A closer examination of some of *Catcher*'s other characters reveals pairs of counterweights that pull Holden in different directions. For example, Mr. Spencer, Holden's history teacher at Pencey, has a counterweight in Mr. Antolini. For Spencer, "[l]ife *is* a game . . . that one plays according to the rules." Spencer's rule-based world seems accusatory, judgmental, and fatalistic, and it repels Holden. Mr. Antolini, by contrast, is "sort of like D.B." and seems to be part of Holden's "recovery" near the end of the weekend. As guide and teacher, he is not fatalistic; his advice is to live and not die for a cause. He serves as a "beautiful reciprocal arrangement" of Holden's learning and later teaching. Similarly, a second dual characterization can be found between two of Holden's dorm-mates at Pencey, Robert Ackley and Stradlater. Both are "slobs," but Ackley is a slob in "personal habits" and Stradlater a "secret" one. Holden's physical self-image seems to fall between the extremes of the "nasty" Ackley (who hates Stradlater) and the "great Stradlater," who is "madly in love with himself." Between these poles of self-revulsion and narcissism, then, Holden tries to locate himself. Yet a third counterweighted characterization is that of Sally Hughes and Jane Gallagher. Jane, like Holden's parents, is an absence that is constantly present. Holden continually tries to get in touch with her, and his image of her is idealized, one of a walled-off princess (she keeps her kings in the back row during checkers, like a wall). Her relationship with Holden is Platonic in the most literal sense of the word—an idealized form with no reality. ("I knew her," Holden says, "like a book.") Sally Hughes, at the opposite pole, is a presence powerfully felt at the beginning of their date, especially in their sexual fumblings in the cab. After the date, though, she becomes an absence: "She wouldn't have been anybody to go with." Here, again, Holden seems to define himself and others through location along a continuum whose end points are personified in the characters who surround him. His self-definition is in reaction to the influences of others, a kind of addition by subtraction, as he fights and flees people and things and then finally learns to embrace the moderation.

The central metaphor of *Catcher*, the "catcher in the rye," appears only near the end of the book and is a kind of symbol-in-motion, a graphic culmination of Holden's frustrations and confusions as he tries to define a self. As a "catcher," he would protect innocence, embrace community, and live in an idyllic and pastoral world. Several critics have noted that this is not the final metaphor helping to define Holden, that he rejects the "catcher" role and becomes at the very end a mere observer of falling, when he lets Phoebe ride the carousel.[5] As catcher or as observer, though, Holden has stopped fighting and fleeing, disguising and disappearing. Neither mania nor depression has won, and he has gained by losing in outgrowing his need for extremes.

Catcher, then, embodies two major themes:

- The social theme is of a self-in-making not fitting into a larger community, whether it is as small as the family or as large as the school and future organizations. Holden embodies a very flawed capacity for social contracture, as do the Glasses, later and in a more extreme form. How much progress that Holden's self makes toward a future integration is one of the enduring questions raised by the book. Is this a rite of passage to adulthood or a declaration not to take part in such a rite? Gerald Rosen has said that Holden is "a prescient portrait of an attempt to create a counterculture."[6] If everyone goes through a developmental process that moves from unquestioning dependence on external institutions and rules to a more sophisticated, internalized set of principles, then where does Holden end up?

- The definition of a self can entail a kind of descent into mental and emotional chaos and even near-madness, a need to fight and to reject (and be rejected by) almost everything and everyone before "catching" and accepting anything. The dynamics of internalizing one's culture can lead to a confusion so complete that no narrative can help, that no resources for survival seem available. Holden's final resource for survival is his acceptance through Phoebe of a permanence/purity in a sibling's nonsexual love, which may lead to a cascade of smaller acceptances (D.B.'s love) and at least a partially healed self. One of the questions raised is whether Holden has lost his innocence at the end and therefore has come to appreciate innocence most having lost it, or whether he has gained another form of innocence. Of course, his saying he "misses" everybody at the end has a double meaning, in that he as narrator may have been inaccurate about everybody, may have "missed" in his descriptions of the world around him.[7] Double meanings of this kind can frustrate or stimulate the reader/audience, or both at once, and Salinger is aware of the importance of both reactions in creating a character and a self.

NINE STORIES (1953)

In one sense, the nine stories are a movie montage, superimposing unrelated events on each other to force a relation between them. Another way of looking at these tentative patterns is to recall Salinger's famous Literary Cubist image, which comes into play in the nine stories—structures that are fragmented to show different angles and different times. Critics have pointed out how many of the nine stories show a character's stunning realization in response to a seemingly small event or object, with some form of resulting enlightenment becoming more apparent in the later stories.[8] Critics also have noted that most of the nine stories recount a search for release from suffering caused by love, loneliness, or some kind of alienation. There may be a thread of children being at risk in some way. To overgeneralize, though, or to try too hard to find patterns among the stories, carries with it an inherent risk of imposing order rather than finding it.

Variations among the stories, however, are clear. Narration may be in the first person or in the third, and some narrators are more trustworthy than others. Sometimes the story starts and ends at the same point, sometimes not. Some endings are neat and provide satisfaction or closure, and some do not. Taken as a whole, the nine stories mark a clear transition from a world only partly touched by the Glass family to the later fiction ruled by the Glasses.

Many have suggested that the famous Zen *koan* at the beginning of the collection, the riddle that admits no easy answer, provides a clue: "We know the sound of two hands clapping. / But what is the sound of one hand clapping?" These stories can be read as riddles without any obvious solutions, and that may be the clearest generalization possible; they are points of departure for thinking, questioning, meditating. Bernice and Sanford Goldstein note that the *koan* experience has two extremes: the struggle to understand can lead to a mental breakdown, or it can result in a form of enlightenment known as *satori*.[9] Gerald Rosen notes that however interesting a *koan* experience may be, it is ultimately something that must be let go of.[10] In any case, the nine *koan* experiences known as the *Nine Stories* seem to require the asking of more and more intelligent questions.

"A Perfect Day for Bananafish"

The narrator of this first story of the collection can be recognized immediately as a detached third person, wanting to report only certain facts—referring to the exact number of advertising men in the hotel and the impersonal "girl in 507" having to wait over two hours to get her call through. The narrator remains cryptic and impersonal throughout. The characters and scenes are introduced in two parts: the first has Muriel Glass in her hotel room finally getting through to her mother and trying to calm fears that Muriel's new husband, Seymour, is dangerously unstable. The second part moves out of the hotel and shows Seymour sitting on the beach, talking to Sybil Carpenter, the four-year-old daughter of a hotel guest. Sybil is clearly unprotected and vulnerable as she plays alone. Given the expectations raised by Muriel's mother, one soon feels a B-movie foreboding as Seymour pushes Sybil out to sea on a raft—to the point where she becomes afraid. Instead of being dangerous, however, Seymour shares in an imaginative fantasy world with Sybil, a world where bananafish swim into a banana hole and eat so much they can't get out. A second expectation of horror is raised when Seymour returns to his hotel room, espies his sleeping bride, and takes a gun from his luggage. That second expectation is twisted as well, when Seymour kills not Muriel but himself.

The reader is left to speculate on the cause of Seymour's suicide. Readers have seen possible causes in his war experiences, and in his realization that he is mismatched with either Muriel or the materialistic bananafish world or both. Whatever the cause, Seymour's suicide becomes one of the central riddles of Salinger's later fiction.

"Uncle Wiggly in Connecticut"

In "Uncle Wiggly," a story of domestic nonbliss, the narrator is, again, a third person, but on a first-name basis with Mary Jane and Eloise (unlike the depersonalization of Muriel in "Bananafish"), former college roommates who are reunited for lunch at Eloise's Connecticut home. Most of the action is conveyed through their dialogue, and the scene is enclosed in the house, only shifting near the end from the living room to the bedroom of Eloise's daughter, Ramona. The landscape framing the house is icy and somewhat menacing, and the neighborhood has "no children at all," excepting Ramona; the setting is a kind of suburbanized wasteland that has confused Mary Jane and taken its toll on Eloise and Ramona.

Eloise has become hardened by her life of frustration and mild estrangement from her husband Lew, her daughter, and others around her. She relives with Mary Jane her relationship with Walt Glass, a mixture of memory and desire that seems to provide some relief from her isolation. Walt was killed during the war when the souvenir stove he was packing for a colonel exploded, a compact symbol-in-action of the threats of military, domestic, and material lives. As they talk, Ramona is left to play outside in the street with her imaginary friend. As in "Bananafish," the expectation of tragedy grows from a child's vulnerability. Here as well something quite different takes place: Ramona's imaginary friend is run over. Later, Eloise explodes with rage at Ramona when she discovers her making room for a new imaginary friend as she goes to bed. Suddenly, however, Eloise clutches Ramona's glasses and dissolves in tears, apparently overcome with the recognition that Ramona's imaginary friend is the emotional equivalent to her memories of Walt Glass. Eloise then makes a gesture of protectiveness toward Ramona by tucking in her blankets and seems to have found a form of consolation and a new resolve.

Critics have explored different meanings in the last lines—from Eloise lapsing into chronic self-pity to her being restored and reunited with her fundamental nature of goodness. John Wenke finds an "unresolved emotional matrix."[11] This emotional riddle may have several answers, and some "right" answers may contradict each other directly; the one hand is still clapping.

"JUST BEFORE THE WAR WITH THE ESKIMOS"

In this third story, the collection's third experiment with variations in narrative voice, the narrator (again in the third person) is neither as detached as in "Bananafish" nor on a first-name basis with the characters, Ginnie Mannox and Selena Graff. The narrator's voice is close to that of Ginnie's, however: "Selena's father made [tennis balls] or something." The primary scene is Selena's apartment, where Ginnie has been annoyed by Selena and has come to be reimbursed for the cab fare for their weekly tennis game. The narrator has access to Ginnie's judgment of the place: "In her opinion, it was an altogether hideous room—expensive but cheesy."

The character of the unprotected and vulnerable "child" has grown somewhat in this story. Selena's brother Franklin, is neither working nor in college, and has a "bad heart." More immediately, Ginnie meets him "bleedin' to death" from a razor blade hidden in a wastebasket. He is among the first of the strikingly unusual characters explored by Salinger in these stories; he is the "funniest-looking boy, or man . . . she had ever seen." Ginnie nurses him through this cut to the bone and helps to nurse him through his description of his failed relationship with her sister. Franklin is about to see Cocteau's *Beauty and the Beast* with a friend, and the parallel with the contrast between Ginnie's "beauty" and his "beast" seems more than accidental. The beast awkwardly offers the beauty a leftover chicken sandwich as a token or gift, and she not only accepts it but also protects it.

As is often the case, the ending invites more than one interpretation. Ginnie may be misplacing her nurturing in what will be a futile relationship, or she may have touched and been touched by Franklin as they healed each other. Evidence supports either "ending;" and there is only a suspension of action, rather than a shaped final circumstance.

"THE LAUGHING MAN"

In this story, for the first time in the collection, a first-person narrator appears, and his exuberant voice is recalling his childhood sense of belonging—to a group known as the Comanche Club and to a story told by the leader of the club, the Chief. The narrator sounds at times like a child living the experiences and at times like a grown man recalling them. The scene shifts from the real playing fields to the imaginary landscapes of the Laughing Man, the main character in the Chief's ongoing story to the children. The Laughing Man was kidnapped by bandits, and his parents left him unprotected by refusing to pay ransom. In a development varied from both *Beauty and the Beast* and Leroux' *The Phantom of the Opera* and incorporating material from detective stories, Westerns, and pirate lore, the Laughing Man has been tortured into having a "horrible face" that he masks with pale red poppy petals as he conducts his wild escapades near the border of China and Paris.

The heroic Chief, telling the story, and the Laughing Man, the story's hero, have parallel lives, one generating and the other amplifying. When the Chief's romance with Mary Hudson ends suddenly and mysteriously, the Laughing Man ceases to be. However, the narrator so vividly remembers each detail of both the story and how he felt when the story was over that he believes he is an ancestor of the Laughing Man. In a sense, he is.

"Down at the Dingy"

This fifth story of the collection has a narrator's voice (again in the third person) that begins by introducing two characters who will "introduce" the two main characters, Boo Boo Tannenbaum (one of the Glass family) and her son Lionel. The scene is another kind of wasteland/"crazy place," a lakeside summer vacation spot with no boats, where no one goes in the water and which contains "lost or abandoned" water skis. Lionel, another in Salinger's troupe of unprotected children, has "been hitting the road regularly since he was two" and appears here floating alone in a dinghy. He is running away from a slur he overheard and does not understand about his father. To rescue and protect him, Boo Boo must reestablish a bond with him that has somehow been broken within the family. She discovers the reason for his flight by entering his imaginative world of pirates and sailors and asserting herself with an "admiral's" special skills and gifts. Boo Boo seems to assure Lionel that he takes precedence with her over his father in a Freudian field day that has Lionel winning a race back to the house.

"For Esmé—With Love and Squalor"

In one of the more complicated stories with its shifting narrators and times, a first-person narrator speaking in the present sounds like the picture of domestic concern and consideration as he puts his mother-in-law ahead of plans to attend a wedding in England that he's "give a lot to be able to get to." He begins to describe a very complex relationship with the bride-to-be, whom he met in England during the war. He recalls his first impression of her: in a church choir where she, Esmé, sings with "the sweetest-sounding, the surest" voice but also has "blasé eyes that . . . might possibly have counted the house." He meets her again later in a tearoom, where she is a relief from the "stale letters" he has from his wife and mother-in-law. A cautiously teasing, almost calculatingly flirtatious Esmé quickly sketches the broad facts of her life (she and her younger brother are orphans, she has a "title," and her parents were mismatched), while the narrator conceals the facts of his own. Charles, her brother, breaks into their conversation and poses a riddle about two walls meeting at a corner, capturing the "meeting" of their perpendicular and not parallel lives that will intersect only once. When Esmé leaves the tearoom, the narrator is "strangely emotional."

In an unusual tactic, the story now shifts from the first-person narration to a third person, Sergeant X. The switch emphasizes a fundamental transformation within the original narrator, who now has gone through the rest of the war and been fragmented in every sense. He is no longer an "I." He is an "X," an unknown. The scene changes as well to a civilian home in Gaufurt, Bavaria in which 10 American soldiers are quartered, a halfway house between war and peace. Sergeant X now is defined by two inscriptions, almost epitaphs: "Dear God, life is hell." "Fathers and teachers, I ponder 'What is hell?' I maintain that it is the suffering of being unable to love." When Sergeant X finally discovers a letter Esmé has written to him, which includes a gift to recall their brief but significant time together (a broken watch), he suddenly discovers or reawakens an ability to love and so at least temporarily ends his hellish suffering. The story ends with his letter responding to her and a return of the "intact" original narrator.

"PRETTY MOUTH AND GREEN MY EYES"

In this story, the most compact of the collection, the detached third-person narrator begins (as in "Bananafish") with no names, only physical descriptions of parts of faces and bodies and gestures. The narrator's voice remains at a distance, never using the names that are revealed in the dialogue, as if the narrator wants to make sure he is not implicated in the affair he is recounting. There is no sense of a physical location. The scene has been reduced to three props: a phone, an ashtray, and a lampshade. In this half-world, narrowed to a phone and some light, exist the lovers, Lee and Joanie, and Joanie's husband, Arthur.

The thematic simplicity of this love triangle is reshaped into a dense and impossible situation as both Lee and Arthur embed truths within lies, revelations within concealments, and friendships within betrayals. Lee's masterful performance in the service of self-protection ultimately sickens him and probably destroys his arrangement with Joanie, who remains a simple and simplified half-person. Arthur's frantic search for Joanie takes him from a need to leave her, to a remembrance of why he loves her, to a lie that might save their marriage. Again, the ending is a suspension of action that leaves open several possibilities from further betrayals to an end of the affair.

"DE DAUMIER-SMITH'S BLUE PERIOD"

This is the longest of the nine stories, and one that seems to have almost reached the critical mass necessary to a full novel. As such, it is the one that gives the narrator the most space and time to develop. He speaks in the first person, recalling events from 13 years before. He begins by acknowledging a force in his life, his late stepfather, Bobby Agadganian, "an adventurous, extremely magnetic, and generous man." The narrator, whose pseudonym is Jean de Daumier-Smith but whose "real" name remains unknown, has "spent so many years laboriously begrudging him those picaresque adjectives" that one suspects this story is a recognition of changes and acceptances over the 13 years since the events it describes. One is prepared for an atonement for past sins and past selves. Jean's parents were divorced when he was eight, and he lived in Paris with his mother and stepfather for many years before Bobby and he returned to New York after his mother's death, when Jean was 19. The move, he says, "threw [him], and threw [him] terribly." Jean's words and actions describe him as an affected, self-absorbed narcissist in the making. He is "elated" at his put-downs of others; he notes his "uncanny physical resemblance to El Greco," lists his art prizes, and completes 18 oil paintings, of which 17 are self-portraits. When Jean applies to become an art instructor at a Canadian correspondence school, he literally makes up his identity from scratch. After joining the school (which sits above an orthopedic appliance shop to imply how close the school's mission is to helping the afflicted, rather than instructing "high, high organized talent"), he gets to sit in judgment of the students. He takes himself so seriously that he can't laugh at one student who lists her favorite artists as Rembrandt and Walt Disney. One suspects that he needs to invent a grand pupil for himself to increase his sense of importance as a master instructor. He chooses Sister Irma.

His pretension finally builds to a breaking point, when he has a two-part conversion experience involving the orthopedic appliance shop that seemingly changes his life. He first has the "hideous" thought that "no matter how coolly or sensibly or gracefully [he] might learn to live [his] life" he "would always be at best a visitor in a garden of enamel urinals and bedpans, with a sightless, wooden dummy-deity standing by in a marked-down rupture truss." The completion of this recognition of the power of experience to diminish the self is his "Experience," a sense that the sun is hurtling at him, which seems to destroy his personal culture of narcissism and allow or force him to let go of the fantasy that he should control the talents and destinies of all Sister Irmas. His need to live in his world of private performances (in reaction to the trauma of losing his mother and life in Paris?) and cultivate an overbearing attention to self seems to vanish at the end of the story, and he rejoins Bobby.

"Teddy"

It may be fitting that the last of the stories is the most riddle-like; the one hand of the *koan* that begins the collection has never clapped so loudly. The narration is in the third person, as that of most of the stories has been, and seems to be only on a formal basis, first with Mr. and Mrs. McArdle and their son Teddy and daughter Booper. The family is returning from Europe on a cruise ship, and the scene changes only by going up and finally down in deck levels; the changing ends at the lowest level, suggesting parallels with Milton's *Paradise Lost*, especially as the narrator gets lost and needs a guide, even then missing the final crucial action. The domestic tensions, between Teddy's mother and father and between Teddy's father and Teddy, don't seem to affect Teddy. He is gazing outward while others are gazing at him, and he says he can't see what emotions are good for, anyway. He is an early incarnation of Seymour Glass, a seer with mystical inclinations/abilities with a "very nice spiritual advancement" that separates him from others even as it makes connections with past and future events, with other nonfinite dimensions. Their nonhuman quality seems to be a separate and alternative human nature either received or achieved, or both.

Teddy soon is shown to have an alternative set of human emotions; he feels an "affinity" for his parents, not a conventional "love." His parents, Teddy explains, don't really *love* their children; "they love their reasons for loving." He refutes a "logical" existence in favor of a nonmaterialistic or transcendent one, further explaining that death simply means getting out of your body one more time in the course of thousands of deaths and rebirths. Teddy seems to be able to predict when people will die, and he predicts his own death as either "today or February 14, 1958." Teddy has a more clearly human counterforce, his sister Booper, who "hates everybody in [the] ocean." He predicts that she may kill him by pushing him into an empty pool, and the final action of the story suggests that this happened. However, the absent narrator can only record a sound; the reader makes the assumptions. If the reader has adopted Teddy's alternative set of emotions and his rejection of "logic," he or she should not be shocked or saddened by whatever has happened—whether Teddy has jumped to his death, been pushed, or pushed Booper. The reader's supposed reaction to the ending indicates just how far he or she is from Teddy's advanced spiritual state. As always, the *koan* has no one answer, only the meditations that lead to more questions.

Franny and Zooey (1961)

Salinger dedicates *Franny and Zooey* to his one-year-old son and to his *New Yorker* editor, William Shawn, asking for acceptance of this "pretty skimpy-looking book." So, at some level, Salinger intended these two stories to be one book fused by the presence of Franny as she is carried through the stages of a three-day emotional and spiritual crisis. Since narrators, narrative voice, characters, and scene vary from one story to the other, it seems as if no one sensibility can narrate a crisis as formidable as Franny's and no one place can hold the people and events as they multiply well beyond the original cast and initial meeting.

The Glasses have now moved in and taken over Salinger's fiction, and they represent "an extended fictional domain."[12] They are a collective cult of personality, embodiments of ego in search of egolessness. Alfred Kazin notes that they are "young, precocious, sensitive, different" and that "[w]hat is ultimate in their love is the love of their own moral and intellectual excellence."[13] However, *Franny and Zooey* has at its core a search for the source of Franny and Zooey's neurosis and guilt, not their love and self-love. One wonders whether Seymour/Buddy programmed them into a freakish search for nonexistence or exposed them to an advanced spiritual self that they can accept or reject.[14]

"Franny"

This story opens with a narrator "zooming in," on characters waiting at a train station, reducing the scope of the narration from twenty or so young men waiting for dates on a football weekend, to six or seven boys out on the platform, then to one boy, Lane Coutell, and finally to a letter that this boy is reading. The letter, to Lane from Franny Glass, expresses a passionate but unbalanced relationship, at once overflowing with pronouncements of love that apparently Lane's most recent letter lacked and also "playfully" declaring disappointment and even hatred. The letter ends with a telling ambiguity: Franny and Lane should, she says, "not try to analyze everything to death for once, if possible, especially me." The meaning of this last phrase shifts between indications that (1) they, and especially Franny, should not analyze *everything* to death and (2) they should not analyze everything, and especially *Franny*, to death. Both happen.

Lane and Franny begin to diverge almost immediately as they bump heads, and his performance of not caring as much as he does is played opposite her performance of caring *more* than she does. His attempts at detachment and hers at attachment move to the main scene, Sickler's (an appropriate name, as Franny will get sick there), and there they escalate their performances into a series of verbal attacks and counterattacks. Franny reacts to the "violence," the failure of their relationship and perhaps in her mind all relationships, with grief spreading later to a physical sickness. Lane reacts by retreating into his meal of snails and frog legs, a comical suggestion of how a lower life form might survive.

Franny tries to defend herself and rise out of and away from the confrontations with her story from "The Way of the Pilgrim," in which a deserving and generous family is taught to pray without ceasing by a wandering pilgrim. Franny has found something and someone she can love and respect in the story, and her true passion for spiritual adventuring takes over. For Lane, this is all "mumbo-jumbo." The story ends with Franny forming soundless words that Lane can't hear, paradoxically fully expressing her crisis in a failed relationship, blocked communication, guilt, destructive self-absorption, and loss of consciousness.

"Zooey"

The story of Franny now becomes transformed. The trajectory of Salinger's last works of fiction now becomes evident as Buddy Glass takes over the narration, complete with a self-conscious and elaborate "author's formal introduction," a redefinition of the short story as a "sort of prose home movie," and a declaration that he is offering not a mystical/religious story, but a love story, "pure and complicated." Buddy argues that "Zooey" is a reconstruction from interviews with Franny, Bessie (mother of Franny and Zooey), and Zooey, thereby going to great lengths to establish the reality and independence of the characters and to give the reader the sense that they are part of a collaborative/performance art form. Buddy seems to indicate the influence, mentioned earlier, that these characters can have on their author *after* their creation. This suggests that the making of fiction had, by the time of this story's writing, begun to spread in Salinger's work as a subject *of* and *for* fiction—just at a time when the mass media were beginning to exert a new pressure on the public. (A comparison might be possible with the effect of the introduction of photography on the fine arts, as the act of painting became a subject *for* painting in response to the more realistic medium of photography.) The narrator of this tale speculates that the story to follow (and implies, by extension, all the Salinger stories to follow) will have little use for "brevity of detail or compression of incident." The shortest distance between any two points will now become a circle, as Salinger's fiction (and that of some other authors) lengthens its details and decompresses its incidents.

After the experiment in "Esmé," the first-person narrator soon changes voice and becomes a third person, a tactic that helps to unify "Zooey" and "Franny." "Zooey" begins on the Monday morning after the miserable weekend of "Franny," in the Manhattan apartment of the Glass family. Franny's crisis has continued, and no help seems forthcoming from her parents—the unusual, vulnerable, unprotected child theme grows up—or from her brother Buddy, to whom she does not have access. Zooey, the youngest Glass son, is not looked at in the family as a force, as a healer, but rather like a beautiful Harlequin mask or a Hollywood starlet—he is lounging in the bathtub reading a four-year-old letter from Buddy, one that is filled with affection and guidance and has been many times reread.

This letter is a prime example of decompression of incident: nothing happens, but much is said. Buddy's letter is an attempt to capture the combined experiences and teachings of Buddy and Seymour in order to instruct and "edify" Zooey, who will complete the transmission to Franny. Buddy and Seymour attempt a systematic but gentle process of disillusionment and subsequent re-illusionment: the performances of a Chekhov play may be "inspired," but they will never be as "beautiful" as Chekhov's talent; education should not begin with a quest for knowledge, but a quest for "no-knowledge"; those between apparent opposites—boys and girls, animals and stones, day and night—are "illusory" differences that religious study can "unlearn." The most direct advice Buddy/Seymour gives is for Zooey to "act, when and where [she] want[s] to." Zooey seems finally to have received the wisdom of the letter, and he now can be prepared to act in a larger sense than simply that of performing.

After the letter-reading, Bessie enters the intimacy of the bathroom, and Zooey and Bessie begin an extended mock combat of verbal sparring that is part mother-son confrontation and part vaudeville routine. Bessie is a life force, a "Queen Mary" to Zooey's "small craft," and she is also the embodiment of daily martyrdom, practical earthliness—clinking with various tools as she walks and "garden[ing]" the medicine cabinet—and the self that neither needs nor wants self-examination. She absorbs his rudeness, and he begins to soften. He is able to describe his rage at being brought up in a very real sense by his brothers and not his parents. He even practices his instructive capabilities by trying to teach Bessie about the protective qualities of Zen ritual and prayer that provide "not exactly an answer" but "[a] response." She is, appropriately, immune to his teachings.

Zooey now takes on the challenge of trying to help Franny. He first uses a combative "siege" that leaves Franny worse, signaling that he still must challenge his own fury and destructiveness before he can help heal both himself and her. Zooey enters a kind of "black box," he goes into Seymour's room after attacking Franny and emerges changed. He literally incorporates the roles of Seymour and Buddy (he pretends to be Buddy, using Seymour's phone), but he also moves beyond them: "We've had enough goddam seers in this family." He also is counterattacked by Franny when she thinks he is Buddy, letting him see the destructive and judgmental version of himself that left her prostrate. He can then finally formulate a form of therapy ("low-grade spiritual counsel") that works: "The only thing you can do now, the only religious thing you can do, is *act*." He has carried the message from Buddy's letter intact to Franny, completing a cycle of healing for both of them. Again, the acting is beyond performing, it is to move beyond the self-examination and self-judgment, to *desire*. It is to live, and live knowing that others are a kind of audience that will give and *for*give: the audience is described as "Christ Himself." Both Franny and Zooey now at least temporarily move beyond a need for the big and blurry fantasies and rituals of incessant prayer that have been a source of power and protection but which also have consumed them. Franny then reaches a joyful state, where the sum of wisdom in the world feels like it is now hers. The ending of the story recalls the narrator's difficulty in expressing transcending, joyful emotions, as opposed to the exhaustingly precise language of pain and despair the expression replaces. As is the case often in Salinger, the closest approximation is "primordial silence" and sleep.

Critics have noted the ironies of Franny's reaching "egolessness" through such an intensive examination of ego and self.[15] How long will the "egoless" state last beyond sleep? Why did an acceptance of the need to "act" so effectively reduce her guilt? Obscuring the true source of the healing and joy in large and blurry fantasy, the story ends posing still more questions.

RAISE HIGH THE ROOF BEAM, CARPENTERS AND SEYMOUR:
AN INTRODUCTION (1963)

This book is the last collection of companion pieces, and contains the two stories about Seymour Glass that originally appeared in 1955 and 1957 in *The New Yorker*. Like those in *Franny and Zooey*, these stories are united by certain elements and divided by others. Buddy Glass is the first-person narrator in both, although he is looking back from a distance of some 20 years in "Raise High the Roof Beam, Carpenters" and is writing in the present tense in "Seymour: An Introduction." Seymour Glass is the main character in both. "Raise High" presents direct evidence of Seymour from his diary, while "Seymour" presents him from summaries of his poetry and memoranda of his critical reactions to Buddy's work. The Seymours that emerge from the two stories can easily be combined into one larger Seymour, but it is one of the great mysteries of Salinger's fiction that readers often are left feeling that they know many other Salinger characters better than they know Seymour, that he is indeed a ghost. Many critics have noted that Seymour's suicide is at the heart of much of Salinger's later fiction. Is Seymour a pure soul rejected by an unenlightened world or a failed guru with an ability to cast spells and make the large blurry fantasies seem like a source of power and protection? Is his death a Teddy-like rejection of the material world or a tragedy undercutting the wisdom of all his teachings? Is he an "addled psychotic" shattered by the war or a soul too pure for this world?[16] Is the Zen Way in all its manifestations The Way, A Way, or No Way? As always, the questions seem more worthy than the answers.

"Raise High the Roof Beam, Carpenters"

Buddy Glass's first few sentences in this story describe a reconfigured family scene in which Seymour Glass and Buddy as teenage boys momentarily become the parents of their sister, Franny, characteristically bypassing her physical nourishment in favor of a Taoist tale—a clear departure from the world of traditional configurations. The tale is about a man worth 10,000 men, a master of "spiritual mechanism" who is able to see inward qualities even as he loses sight of the external. Buddy equates this man with Seymour, and then tells the story of Seymour's wedding day in 1942.

Buddy has been enlisted as the only member of the Glass family who can go the wedding, and again traditional configurations are skewed: the young soldier Buddy arrives crippled with pleurisy and eventually finds the enormous old brownstone (not church or temple) that will house the wedding. Then, there is no wedding, apparently because the groom, Seymour, is too happy to get married. The guests are evacuated with paramilitary maneuvers, and Buddy comically ends up in a cab with the Matron of Honor, who is "bayonetlike" and "bloodthirsty." He must become a secret agent for as long as possible out of fear of reprisals. In this combative world where externals seem strange and reversed, Seymour is the center of everything. This is a narrative of counter-intuition, and events are fractured and uncommon. Expectations are defeated.

The wedding does indeed take place, as an elopement, later that day, and the former combatants in the cab find themselves at Buddy and Seymour's apartment, where Buddy as reluctant host himself disappears from the party to read from Seymour's diary. The diary shows a Seymour not worried that his bride's love for him "comes and goes, appears and disappears" and a willing resignation to the fact that she "loves [him], but she'll never feel really close to [him], *familiar* with [him], *frivolous* with [him], 'till [he's] slightly overhauled." This is a recasting of Teddy's statement that his parents "don't seem able to love [their children] unless they can keep changing [them] a little bit," a pure expression of conditional parental love that now appears as a pure expression of conditional romantic love. In keeping with the "spiritual mechanism" exhibited in the Taoist tale, Seymour ignores the external, i.e., Muriel's conditional love. He is intent on the inward qualities—he is blissfully happy with Muriel and her "undiscriminating heart."

Just as there can be some difficulty at times in identifying the precise source of the other Glass's pain at any given moment, given what the narrator tells and what he withholds, there can be some difficulty also, at times, in identifying the precise source of Seymour's joy. Seymour has either received or achieved a predisposition toward happiness. He even diagnoses himself as a "paranoiac in reverse"; he "suspect[s] people of plotting to make [him] happy." That ambiguity is at the center of the character; his "paranoia in reverse" can be interpreted as a belief either that people are plotting for his happiness but not succeeding or that people are the source of his happiness because of their deliberate efforts. He also identifies the "joy of responsibility" that he will feel after the marriage, in accordance with Zen dictates. The failure of language to capture Zen-like truths becomes even more evident here. The ending of "Raise High" moves toward an understanding of Seymour that is colored by the knowledge that he will commit suicide. Comprehension requires either the ultimate unconventional reconfiguration, i.e., an understanding of that suicide as an act of joy and fulfillment, or suspicion of the paths to joy that he has laid out.[17] Buddy states explicitly that he will be of no help; he will leave a blank piece of paper by way of explanation.

"SEYMOUR: AN INTRODUCTION"

This story, the other half of *Raise High*, begins with passages from Kafka and Kierkegaard, which notify the reader that the writer's relationship to his characters will be central to the plot. The first lines from Buddy add that the relationship of the writer to the reader will also be studied. In other words, the fiction has turned inward to look at the "spiritual mechanism" in writing and reading, and this introspection will come at the expense of the externals or conventions of narration, characters, and plot. The study of mechanics will even get down to the details of what the symbols on a page are signifying: Buddy offers a "bouquet of early-blooming parentheses: (((( ))))" as a gift to the reader as his "deeply contemporary confidant."

"Seymour" is a virtual incubator of plot fragments, character ideas, random thoughts, poetic images, and extended metaphors. It is a chaotic warehouse of artistic activity, and to wander therein is both gratifying and stupefying. It is also an extended data-gathering session on the part of Buddy, an attempt to get credible information about artistic processes that may not be handed down from others. He wants to trace the cycles of ecstasy and despair; at various points in the story, Buddy is ecstatic, or dismayed and disgusted, sitting in a "horrible chair." He seems to be creating a kind of narrative Heisenberg uncertainty principle, since the events he records change *because* he records them. One can know a character's trajectory or its "essence" but never both.

Buddy seems to create at least three main abstractions or characters in "Seymour": the artist/writer as Sick Man; the meta-character, a compilation of many other characters in Salinger's fiction; and the audience. The artist/writer, Buddy says, is a Sick Man who "gives out terrible cries of pain, as if he would wholeheartedly let go both his art and his soul to experience what passes in other people for wellness" and yet lets the sickness run its course because it is a source of art. The source of the sickness, pain, and eventual death is the artist's "own scruples, the blinding shapes and colors of his own sacred human conscience." The two opening passages elaborate on this; taken together, they construct the cause of the artist/writer's sickness as the knowledge that the characters are necessarily flawed by the process of creating them and that they are beings the collective world gets to re-create as its own. The less skillfully the artist/writer/seer has performed the creation, the more the characters depend on the *audience* to create them, an "unholy collaboration." The more a writer "loves" a character, and the more clearly that character is rendered, the more the artist is frustrated by his inability to change his own creation. He has to accept it, endure it, maintain its consistency, and never falsify it.

Buddy also creates in "Seymour" a kind of meta-character, a combination of other characters that Buddy claims to have created in his other work; these represent either a key to his main characters, or a kind of joke on the act of trying to distill characters—each is possible. Buddy outlines his meta-characters: they "speak Manhattanese fluently and idiomatically"; they "have a rather common flair for rushing in where most fools fear to tread"; they are "pursued by an Entity." Mapping Holden, the Glasses, and others onto this grid may be an exercise some readers will want to try, and Buddy invites them to do so, at their own peril.

The third character Seymour creates in this story is the audience or reader. The reader is his "confidant," to whom he is "liberated" to tell all; and before the reader he will pull no more tricks. The magician is letting out his secrets. Buddy tells the members of his audience that they come in three varieties, reducing *them* to types, just as they, when reading, tend to categorize *characters*: "the young man or woman who loves and respects to distraction any fairly responsible sort of literature"; "the kind of young person who actually rings doorbells in the pursuit of literary data"; those who want to equate the artist with the creation and are curious about the artist. Enthusiasts, Academics, and the Curious. Mapping oneself onto this supplied grid is as tedious as mapping Salinger's characters to the grid above. However, Buddy is nothing if not filled with categories and types. He is acting as both writer and reader.

Unexpectedly, the one character that seems to recede in "Seymour" is Seymour. Buddy has taken over, and his "portrait of Seymour remains unformulated and incomplete, because he cannot discriminate among his memories."[18] Buddy as sorcerer's apprentice now feels he must provide even more "keys" to the "kingdom" of the artist/writer/seer. Extrapolating from his description of Seymour's poems, one sees that the artist/writer/seer has made structural and tonal choices: Seymour/Buddy has been working inside "attractive restricted areas" such as the short story or haiku; each work is "unsonorous . . . but there are intermittent short blasts of euphony"; the tone is "not light- but high-hearted"; the works "can be read by anyone . . . but [he] wouldn't . . . recommend the last [works]....to any living soul who hasn't died at least twice in his lifetime, preferably slowly." These secret recipes for cooking fiction seem to exhaust Buddy, and he goes to bed several times in the course of revealing them.

Ultimately, Buddy suspends the story. He returns to the people who shine more than anyone—his students. Reading this, one knows one was among the last people Buddy and Salinger wanted to address.

The reader in "Seymour," and throughout Salinger's oeuvre, lives with an artist and his narrative problems and solutions and realizes the necessity of continuing to ask the questions that Salinger cannot be expected to answer. Salinger's characters work out an uneasy and inconclusive salvation that does not attempt to lead to a better collective future for those outside the family; fortunately, the reader may be part of that family.

NOTES

1. Paul Alexander, *Salinger: A Biography*. Los Angeles: Renaissance Books, 1999, p. 167.

2. Daniel Boorstin, *The Americans*. New York: Random House, 1965, pp. 307–324.

3. Gerald Rosen, "A Retrospective Look at *The Catcher in the Rye*," *J.D. Salinger: Modern Critical Views*, ed. Harold Bloom. Philadelphia: Chelsea House Publishers, 1987, p. 106.

4. Susan K. Mitchell, "Holden Caulfield: An Unreliable Narrator," *Readings on* The Catcher in the Rye, ed. Steven Engel. San Diego: Greenhaven Press, 1998, p. 63.

5. Sanford Pinsker, *The Catcher in the Rye: Innocence Under Pressure*. New York: Twayne, 1993.

6. Rosen, p. 108.

7. James Lundquist, *J.D. Salinger*. New York: Ungar, 1979, p. 52.

8. John Wenke, *J.D. Salinger: A Study of the Short Fiction*. Boston: Twayne, 1991, p. 34.

9. Bernice Goldstein and Sanford Goldstein, "Zen and *Nine Stories*," *J.D. Salinger: Modern Critical Views*, ed. Harold Bloom. Philadelphia: Chelsea House Publishers, 1987, p. 82.

10. Rosen, p. 109.

11. Wenke, p. 41.

12. Wenke, p. 63.

13. Alfred Kazin, "J.D. Salinger: 'Everybody's Favorite,'" *J.D. Salinger: Modern Critical Views*, ed. Harold Bloom. Philadelphia: Chelsea House Publishers, 1987, p. 25.

14. Wenke, p. 80.

15. Wenke, p. 67.

16. Wenke, p. 65.

17. Max F. Schulz, "Salinger and the Crisis of Consciousness," *J.D. Salinger: Modern Critical Views*, ed. Harold Bloom. Philadelphia: Chelsea House Publishers, 1987.

18. Schulz, p. 55.

ALFRED KAZIN

J.D.Salinger: "Everybody's Favorite"

The publication of his two well-known stories from the *New Yorker* in book form, *Franny and Zooey* (Little, Brown), brings home the fact that, for one reason or another, J.D. Salinger now figures in American writing as a special case. After all, there are not many writers who could bring out a book composed of two stories—both of which have already been read and argued over and analyzed to death by that enormous public of sophisticated people which radiates from the *New Yorker* to every English department in the land. Yet Salinger's fascination for this public is so great that, although he has refused this book to every book club, it may yet sell as if it were being pushed by book clubs. Since 1953, when *The Catcher in the Rye* was reprinted as a paperback, it has become the favorite American novel on the required or suggested reading lists of American colleges and secondary schools, and it has sold well over a million and a half copies. No less unusual is the fact that the *New Yorker*—which, if it did not originate, certainly brought to perfection the kind of tight, allusive, ironic story with which Salinger's earlier stories (reprinted in *Nine Stories*, 1953) felt so much at home—published in "Zooey" (41,130 words) the longest story it had ever published, and a story for which the *New Yorker* obviously felt personal affection and some particular intellectual sympathy.

In one form or another, as a fellow novelist commented unlovingly, Salinger is "everybody's favorite." He is certainly a favorite of the *New Yorker*,

From *The Atlantic Monthly* 208, no. 2 (August 1961). © 1961 by Alfred Kazin. Reprinted by permission.

which in 1959 published another long story around the Glass family called "Seymour: An Introduction" (almost 30,000 words), and thus gave the impression of stretching and remaking itself to Salinger's latest stories, which have been appearing, like visits from outer space, at two-year intervals. But above all, he is a favorite with that audience of students, student intellectuals, instructors, and generally literary, sensitive, and sophisticated young people who respond to him with a consciousness that he speaks for them and virtually *to* them, in a language that is peculiarly honest and their own, with a vision of things that capture their most secret judgments of the world. The only thing that Salinger does not do for this audience is to meet with them. Holden Caulfield said in *The Catcher in the Rye* that "What really knocks me out is a book that, when you're all done reading it, you wish the author that wrote it was a terrific friend of yours and you could call him up on the phone whenever you felt like it." It is well for him that all the people in this country who now regard J.D. Salinger as a "terrific friend" do not call him up and reach him.

A fundamental reason for Salinger's appeal (like that of Hemingway in the short stories that made *him* famous) is that he has exciting professional mastery of a peculiarly charged and dramatic medium, the American short story. At a time when so much American fiction has been discursive in tone, careless in language, lacking in edge and force—when else would it have been possible for crudities like the Beat novelists to be taken seriously?— Salinger has done an honest and stimulating professional job in a medium which, when it is expertly handled, projects emotion like a cry from the stage and in form can be as intense as a lyric poem. A short story which is not handled with necessary concentration and wit is like a play which does not engage its audience; a story does not exist unless it hits its mark with terrific impact. It is a constant projection of meanings at an audience, and it is a performance minutely made up of the only possible language, as a poem is. In America, at least, where, on the whole, the best stories are the most professional stories and so are published in the most famous magazines, second-rate stories belong in the same limbo with unsuccessful musical comedies; unless you hit the bull's-eye, you don't score.

This does not mean that the best-known stories are first-rate pieces of literature any more than that so many triumphant musical comedies are additions to the world's drama; it means only that a story has communicated itself with entire vividness to its editor and its audience. The profundity that may exist in a short story by Chekhov or Tolstoy also depends upon the author's immediate success in conveying his purpose. Even in the medieval tale, which Tolstoy in his greatest stories seems to recapture in tone and spirit, the final comment on human existence follows from the deliberate artlessness of tone that the author has managed to capture like a speech in a play.

What makes Salinger's stories particularly exciting is his intense, his almost compulsive need to fill in each inch of his canvas, each moment of his scene. Many great novels owe their grandeur to a leisurely sense of suggestion, to the imitation of life as a boundless road or flowing river, to the very relaxation of that intensity which Poe thought was the aesthetic perfection of a poem or a story. But whatever the professional superficiality of the short story in American hands, which have molded and polished it so as to reach, dazzle, and on occasion deceive the reader, a writer like Salinger, by working so hard to keep his tiny scene alive, keeps everything humming. Someday there will be learned theses on "The Use of the Ash Tray in J.D. Salinger's Stories"; no other writer has made so much of Americans lighting up, reaching for the ash tray, setting up the ash tray with one hand while with the other they reach for a ringing telephone. Ours is a society complicated with many appliances, and Salinger always tells you what his characters are doing with each of their hands. In one long stretch of "Zooey," he describes that young man sitting in a bathtub, reading a long letter from his brother, and smoking; he manages to describe every exertion made and every sensation felt in that bathtub by the young man whose knees made "dry islands." Then the young man's mother comes into the bathroom; he draws the shower curtains around the tub, she rearranges the medicine cabinet, and while they talk (in full), everything they do is described. Everything, that is, within Salinger's purpose in getting at such detail, which is not the loose, shuffling catalogue of the old-fashioned naturalists, who had the illusion of reproducing the whole world, but the tension of a dramatist or theater director making a fuss about a character's walking just so.

For Salinger, the expert performer and director (brother Buddy Glass, who is supposed to be narrating "Zooey," speaks of "directing" it and calls the story itself a "prose home movie"), gesture is the essence of the medium. A short story does not offer room enough for the development of character; it can present only character itself, by gesture. And Salinger is remarkable, I would say he is almost frenetically proficient, in getting us, as the opening of "Franny," to *see* college boys waiting on a train platform to greet their dates arriving for a big football weekend. They rush out to the train, "most of them giving the impression of having at least three lighted cigarettes in each hand." He knows exactly how Franny Glass would be greeted by Lane Coutell: "It was a station-platform kiss—spontaneous enough to begin with, but rather inhibited in the follow-through, and with something of a forehead-bumping aspect."

And ever better is his description of the boy at a good restaurant, taking a first sip of his martini and then looking "around the room with an almost palpable sense of well-being at finding himself (he must have been sure no one could dispute) in the right place with an unimpeachably right-looking girl." Salinger knows how to prepare us with this gesture for the later insensitivity of a boy who is exactly one of those elaborately up-to-date and anxiously sophisticated people whom Franny Glass, pure in heart, must learn to tolerate, and even to love, in what she regards as an unbearably shallow culture.

But apart from this, which is the theme of *Franny and Zooey*, the gesture itself is recognized by the reader not only as a compliment to himself but as a sign that Salinger is working all the time, not merely working to get the reader to see, but working to make his scene itself hum with life and creative observation. I don't know how much this appearance of intensity on the part of Salinger, of constant as well as full coverage, is due to *New Yorker* editorial nudging, since its famous alertness to repetitions of words and vagueness of diction tends to give an external look of freshness and movement to prose. Salinger not only works very hard indeed over each story, but he obviously writes to and for some particular editorial mind he identifies with the *New Yorker*; look up the stories he used to write for the *Saturday Evening Post* and *Cosmopolitan*, and you will see that just as married people get to look alike by reproducing each other's facial expressions, so a story by Salinger and passage of commentary in the *New Yorker* now tend to resemble each other.

But whatever the enormous influence of any magazine on those who write regularly for it, Salinger's emphasis of certain words and syllables in American speech and his own compulsiveness in bearing down hard on certain details (almost as if he wanted to make the furniture, like the gestures of certain people, tell *everything* about the people who use them) do give his stories the intensity of observation that is fundamental to his success. Lane Coutell, sitting in that restaurant with Franny and talking about a college paper on Flaubert he is horribly well satisfied with, says,

> I think the emphasis I put on *why* he was so neurotically attached to the *mot juste* wasn't too bad. I mean in the light of what we know today. Not just psychoanalysis and all that crap, but certainly to a certain extent. You know what I mean. I'm no Freudian man or anything like that, but certain things you can't just pass over as capital-F Freudian and let them go at that. I mean to a certain extent I think I was perfectly justified to point out that none of the really good boys—Tolstoy, Dostoevski, *Shake*speare, for Chrissake—were such goddam word-squeezers. They just wrote. Know what I mean?

What strikes me about this mimicry is not merely that it is so clever, but that it is also so relentless. In everything that this sophisticated ass, Lane Coutell, says, one recognizes that he is and will be wrong. Salinger disapproves of him in the deepest possible way; he is a spiritual enemy.

Of course, it is a vision of things that lies behind Salinger's expert manner. There is always one behind every manner. The language of fiction, whatever it may accomplish as representation, ultimately conveys an author's intimation of things; makes us hear, not in a statement, but in the ensemble of his realized efforts, his quintessential commentary on the nature of existence. However, the more deliberate the language of the writer, as it must be in a short story, the more the writer must convey his judgment of things in one highlighted dramatic action, as is done on the stage.

At the end of "Franny," the young girl collapses in the ladies' room of the restaurant where she has been lunching with her cool boyfriend. This conveys her spiritual desperation in his company, for Lane typifies a society where "Everything everybody does is so—I don't know—not *wrong*, or even mean, or even stupid necessarily. But just so tiny and meaningless and—sad-making." Her brother Zooey (Zachary Glass), at the end of the long second story, calls her up from another telephone number in the same apartment and somehow reaches to the heart of her problem and gives her peace by reminding her that the "Fat Lady" they used to picture somnolently listening to them when they were quiz kids on the radio—the ugly, lazy, even disgusting-looking Fat Lady, who more and more typifies unattractive and selfish humanity in our day—can be loved after all, for she, too, is Jesus Christ.

In each story, the climax bears a burden of meaning that it would not have to bear in a novel; besides being stagy, the stories are related in a way that connects both of them into a single chronicle. This, to quote the title of a little religious pamphlet often mentioned in it, might be called "The Way of a Pilgrim." Both Franny and Zooey Glass are, indeed, pilgrims seeking their way in a society typified by the Fat Lady, and even by Lane Coutell's meaningless patter of sophistication. No wonder Franny cries out to her unhearing escort: "I'm sick of just liking people. I wish to God I could meet somebody I could respect." The Glasses (mother Irish, father Jewish) are ex-vaudevillians whose children were all, as infant prodigies, performers on a radio quiz program called "It's a Wise Child." Now, though engaged in normally sophisticated enterprises (Franny goes to a fashionable women's college, Zooey is a television actor, Buddy a college instructor), they have retained their intellectual precocity—and, indeed, their precocious charm—and have translated, as it were, their awareness of themselves as special beings into a conviction that they alone can do justice to their search for the true way.

The eldest and most brilliant of the children, Seymour, shot himself in 1948 while on his honeymoon in Florida; this was the climax of Salinger's perhaps most famous story, "A Perfect Day for Bananafish." And it is from Seymour's old room in the Glass apartment that Zooey calls up his sister, Franny, on a phone that is normally never used, that is still listed in the name of Seymour Glass, and that has been kept up by Buddy (who does not want a phone in his own country retreat) and by Zooey in order to perpetuate Seymour's name and to symbolize his continuing influence on them as a teacher and guide. It is from reading over again, in Seymour's old room, various religious sayings from the world's literature that Seymour had copied out on a piece of beaverboard nailed to the back of a door that Zooey is inspired to make the phone call to Franny that ends with the revelation that the horrible Fat Lady is really Jesus Christ.

This final episode, both in the cuteness of its invention and in the cuteness of speech so often attributed to Seymour, who is regarded in his own family as a kind of guru, or sage, helps us to understand Salinger's wide popularity. I am sorry to have to use the word "cute" in respect to Salinger, but there is absolutely no other word that for me so accurately typifies the self-conscious charm and prankishness of his own writing and his extraordinary cherishing of his favorite Glass characters.

Holden Caulfield is also cute in *The Catcher in the Rye*, cute in his little-boy suffering for his dead brother, Allie, and cute in his tenderness for his sister, "Old Phoebe." But we expect that boys of that age may be cute—that is, consciously appealing and consciously clever. To be these things is almost their only resource in a world where parents and schoolmasters have all the power and the experience. Cuteness, for an adolescent, is to turn the normal self-pity of children, which arises from their relative weakness, into a relative advantage vis-à-vis the adult world. It becomes a role boys can play in the absence of other advantages, and *The Catcher in the Rye* is so full of Holden's cute speech and cute innocence and cute lovingness for his own family that one must be an absolute monster not to like it.

And on a higher level, but with the same conscious winsomeness, the same conscious mournfulness and intellectual loneliness and lovingness (though not for his wife), Seymour Glass is cute when he sits on the beach with a little girl telling her a parable of "bananafish"—ordinary-looking fish when "they swim into a hole where there's a lot of bananas," but "after that they're so fat they can't get out of the hole again. . . . They die." His wife, meanwhile busy in their room on the long-distance phone to her mother in New York, makes it abundantly clear in the hilariously accurate cadences and substance of her conversation why her husband finds it more natural to talk to a four-year-old girl on the beach than to her. Among other things,

Seymour expects not to be understood outside the Glass family. But agonizing as this situation is, the brilliantly entertaining texture of "A Perfect Day for Bananafish" depends on Seymour Glass's conscious cleverness as well as on his conscious suffering—even his conscious cleverness *about* the suffering or "ordinary-looking" fish who get so bloated eating too many bananas in a "hole" they shouldn't have been attracted to in the first place.

In the same way, not only does the entertaining surface of *Franny and Zooey* depend on the conscious appealingness and youthfulness and generosity and sensitivity of Seymour's brother and sister, but Salinger himself, in describing these two, so obviously feels such boundless affection for them that you finally get the sense of all these child prodigies and child entertainers being tied round and round with veils of self-love in a culture which they—and Salinger—just despise. Despise, above all, for its intellectual pretentiousness. Yet this is the society, typified by the Fat Lady (symbolically, they pictured her as their audience), whom they must now force themselves to think of as Jesus Christ, and whom, as Christ Himself, they can now at last learn to love.

For myself, I must confess that the spiritual transformation that so many people associate with the very sight of the word "love" on the printed pages does not move me as it should. In what has been considered Salinger's best story, "For Esmé—With Love and Squalor," Sergeant X in the American Army of Occupation in Germany is saved from a hopeless breakdown by the beautiful magnanimity and remembrance of an aristocratic young English girl. We are prepared for this climax or visitation by an earlier scene in which the sergeant comes upon a book by Goebbels in which a Nazi woman had written, "Dear God, life is hell." Under this, persuaded at last of his common suffering even with a Nazi, X writes down, from *The Brothers Karamazov*: "Fathers and teachers, I ponder 'What is hell?' I maintain that it is the suffering of being unable to love."

But the love that Father Zossima in Dostoyevski's novel speaks for is surely love for the world, for God's creation itself, for all that precedes us and supports us, that will outlast us and that alone helps us to explain ourselves to ourselves. It is the love that D. H. Lawrence, another religious novelist, spoke of as "the sympathetic bond" and that in one form or another lies behind all the great novels as a primary interest in everyone and everything alive with us on this common earth. The love that Salinger's horribly precocious Glass characters speak of is love for certain people only— forgiveness is for the rest; finally, through Seymour Glass's indoctrination of his brothers and sister in so many different (and pretentiously assembled) religious teachings, it is love of certain ideas. So what is ultimate in their love is the love of their own moral and intellectual excellence, of their chastity and purity in a world full of bananafish swollen with too much food. It is the love that they have for themselves as an idea.

The worst they can say about our society is that they are too sensitive to live in it. They are the special case in whose name society is condemned. And what makes them so is that they are young, precocious, sensitive, different. In Salinger's work, the two estates—the world and the cutely sensitive young—never really touch at all. Holden Caulfield condemns parents and school because he knows that they are incapable of understanding him; Zooey and Franny and Buddy (like Seymour before them) know that the great mass of prosperous spiritual savages in our society will never understand them.

This may be true, but to think so can lead to a violation of art. Huckleberry Finn, so often cited as a parallel to the hero of *The Catcher in the Rye*, was two years younger than Holden, but the reason he was not afraid of an adult's world is that he had respect for it. He had never even seen very much of it until he got on that raft with a runaway Negro slave he came to love and was able to save. It was still all God's creation, and inspired him with wonder. But Holden and, even more, the Glass children are beaten before they start; beaten in order not to start. They do not trust anything or anyone but themselves and their great idea. And what troubles me about this is not what is reflects of their theology but what it does to Salinger's art.

Frank O'Connor once said of this special métier, the short story, that it is "the art form that deals with the individual when there is no longer a society to absorb him, and when he is compelled to exist, as it were, by his own inner light." This is the condition on which Salinger's work rests, and I should be sorry to seem unsympathetic toward it. It is an American fact, as one can see from the relative lack in our literature of the ripe and fully developed social novel in which the individual and society are in concrete and constant relationship with each other. But whatever this lack, which in one sense is as marked in the novels of Scott Fitzgerald as it is in Salinger's emphasis upon the short story, it is a fact that when Fitzgerald describes a character's voice, it is because he really loves—in the creative sense, is fully interested in—this character. When Salinger describes a character's voice, it is to tell us that the man is a phony. He has, to borrow a phrase from his own work, a "categorical aversion" to whole classes and types of our society. The "sympathetic bond" that Lawrence spoke of has been broken. People stink in our nostrils. We are mad with captious observation of one another. As a friend of mine once said about the novels of Mary McCarthy, trying to say with absolute justice what it was that shocked her so much in them, "The heroine is always right and everyone else is wrong." Salinger is a far more accomplished and objective writer of fiction than Mary McCarthy, but I would say that in his work the Glass children alone are right and everyone else is wrong.

And it is finally this condition, not just the famous alienation of Americans from a society like our own, that explains the popularity of Salinger's work. Salinger's vast public, I am convinced, is based not merely on the vast number of young people who recognize their emotional problems in his fiction and their frustrated rebellions in the sophisticated language he manipulates so skillfully. It is based perhaps even more on the vast numbers who have been released by our society to think of themselves as endlessly sensitive, spiritually alone, gifted, and whose suffering lies in the narrowing of their consciousness to themselves, in the withdrawal of their curiosity from a society which they think they understand all too well, in the drying up of their hope, their trust, and their wonder at the great world itself. The worst of American sophistication today is that it is so bored, so full of categorical aversion to things that writers should never take for granted and never close their eyes to.

The fact that Salinger's work is particularly directed against the "well fed sun-burned" people at the summer theater, at the "section men" in colleges parroting the latest fashionable literary formulas, at the "three-martini" men—this, indeed, is what is wrong. He hates them. They are no longer people, but symbols, like the Fat Lady. No wonder that Zooey tells his sister: Love them, love them all, love them anyway! But the problem is not one of spiritual pride or of guilt; it is that in the tearing of the "sympathetic bond" it is not love that goes, but the deepest possibilities of literary art.

STEPHEN J. WHITFIELD

Cherished and Cursed: Toward a Social History of The Catcher in the Rye

The plot is brief: in 1949 or perhaps 1950, over the course of three days during the Christmas season, a sixteen-year-old takes a picaresque journey to his New York City home from the third private school to expel him. The narrator recounts his experiences and opinions from a sanitarium in California. A heavy smoker, Holden Caulfield claims to be already six feet, two inches tall and to have wisps of grey hair; and he wonders what happens to the ducks when the ponds freeze in winter. The novel was published on 16 July 1951, sold for $3.00, and was a Book-of-the-Month Club selection. Within two weeks, it had been reprinted five times, the next month three more times—though by the third edition the jacket photograph of the author had quietly disappeared. His book stayed on the bestseller list for thirty weeks, though never above fourth place.[1]

Costing 75 cents, the Bantam paperback edition appeared in 1964. By 1981, when the same edition went for $2.50, sales still held steady, between twenty and thirty thousand copies per month, about a quarter of a million copies annually. In paperback the novel sold over three million copies between 1953 and 1964, climbed even higher by the 1980s, and continues to attract about as many buyers as it did in 1951. The durability of its appeal is astonishing. *The Catcher in the Rye* has gone through over seventy printings and has spread into thirty languages. Three decades after it first appeared, a mint copy of the first edition was already fetching about $200.[2]

From *The New England Quarterly*, v. 70, no. 4, December 1997, pp. 567–600, for "Cherished and cursed: Toward a social history of *The Catcher in the Rye*" by Stephen J. Whitfield. Copyright held by *The New England Quarterly*. Reproduced by permission of the publisher and the author.

Critical and academic interest has been less consistent; and how J.D. Salinger's only novel achieved acclaim is still a bit mystifying. After its first impact came neglect: following the book reviews, only three critical pieces appeared in the first five years. In the next four years, at least seventy essays on *The Catcher in the Rye* were published in American and British magazines. Salinger's biographer explained why: "A feature of the youthquake was, of course, that students could now tell their teachers what to read." Ian Hamilton also notes that by the mid-1950s the novel had "become the book all brooding adolescents had to buy, [and on campuses] the indispensable manual from which cool styles of disaffection could be borrowed."[3] No American writer over the past half-century has entranced serious young readers more than Salinger, whose novel about the flight from Pencey Prep may lag behind only *Of Mice and Men* on public-school required reading lists.[4] And his fiction has inspired other writers as well; the late Harold Brodkey, for example, considered it "the most influential body of work in English prose by anyone since Hemingway." [5]

One explanation for why *The Catcher in the Rye* has enjoyed such a sustained readership came over two decades after the novel was first published—from a middle-aged Holden Caulfield himself, as imagined by journalist Stefan Kanfer: "The new audience is never very different from the old Holden. They may not know the words, but they can hum along with the malady. My distress is theirs. They, too, long for the role of adolescent savior. They, too, are aware of the imminent death in life. As far as the sexual explosion is concerned, I suspect a lot of what you've heard is just noise." Sex "still remains a mystery to the adolescent. I have no cure, only consolation: someone has passed this way before." Objections to schlock and vulgarity and physical decline, and preferences for the pastoral over the machine continue to resonate, "Holden" suspects;[6] and so long as the United States continues to operate very much this side of paradise, a reluctance to inherit what the grown-ups have bequeathed is bound to enlist sympathy. The fantasy of withdrawal and retreat to the countryside ("Massachusetts and Vermont, and all around there . . . [are] beautiful as hell up there. It really is.") is not only a commonplace yearning but also advice Holden's creator elected to take by moving to Cornish, New Hampshire.[7]

But it should be conceded that generally it's the grown-ups who are in charge, and many of them have wanted to ban the widely beloved novel. Why *The Catcher in the Rye* has been censored (and censured) as well as cherished is a curiosity worth examining for its own sake. But how so transparently charming a novel can also exercise a peculiar allure and even emit disturbing danger signals may serve as an entree into postwar American culture as well.

Bad Boys, Bad Readers

One weird episode inspired by *The Catcher in the Rye* involves Jerry Lewis. He tried to buy the movie rights, which were not for sale, and to play the lead. One problem was that the director did not read the book until the 1960s, when he was already well into his thirties. Playing the protagonist would have been a stretch, but le roi de crazy felt some affinity for Salinger (whom Lewis never met): "He's nuts also." Curiously Holden himself mentions the word "crazy" and its cognates (like "mad," "madman," and "insane") over fifty times, more than the reverberant "phony."[8]

Indeed the history of this novel cannot be disentangled from the way the mentally unbalanced have read it. In one instance the reader is himself fictional: the protagonist of John Fowles's first book, which captures the unnerving character of Salinger's only novel as an index of taste, perhaps of moral taste. In the second section of *The Collector*, told from the viewpoint of the victim, the kidnapped Miranda Grey recounts in her diary that she asks her captor, lepidopterist Frederick Clegg, whether he reads "proper books—real books." When he admits that "light novels are more my line," she recommends *The Catcher in the Rye* instead: "I've almost finished it. Do you know I've read it twice and I'm five years younger than you are?" Sullenly he promises to read it. Later she notices him doing so, "several times . . . look[ing] to see how many pages more he had to read. He reads it only to show me how hard he is trying." After the duty has been discharged, over a week later, the collector admits: "I don't see much point in it." When Miranda counters, "You realize this is one of the most brilliant studies of adolescence ever written?" he responds that Holden "sounds a mess to me." "Of course he's a mess. But he realizes he's a mess, he tries to express what he feels, he's a human being for all his faults. Don't you even feel sorry for him?"

"I don't like the way he talks."

"I don't like the way you talk," she replies. "But I don't treat you as below any serious notice or sympathy."

Clegg acknowledges: "I suppose it's very clever. To write like that and all."

"I gave you that book to read because I thought you would feel identified with him. You're a Holden Caulfield. He doesn't fit anywhere and you don't."

"I don't wonder, the way he goes on. He doesn't try to fit."

Miranda insists: "He tries to construct some sort of reality in his life, some sort of decency."

"It's not realistic. Going to a posh school and his parents having money. He wouldn't behave like that. In my opinion."

She has the final word (at least in her diary): "You get on the back of everything vital, everything trying to be honest and free, and you bear it down."

Modern art, she realizes, embarrasses and fascinates Clegg; it "shocks him" and stirs "guilty ideas in him" because he sees it as "all vaguely immoral." For the mass audience at which William Wyler's 1965 film adaptation was aimed, Clegg's aesthetic world is made less repellent and more conventional, and the conversation about *The Catcher in the Rye* is abbreviated. [9]

In a more class-conscious society than is the United States, Fowles's loner finds something repugnant about the recklessness of the privileged protagonist. In a more violent society than England, types like Frederick Clegg might identify with Holden Caulfield's alienation from "normal" people so thoroughly that they become assassins. To be sure, *The Catcher in the Rye* is bereft of violence; and no novel seems less likely to activate the impulse to "lock and load." But this book nevertheless has exercised an eerie allure for asocial young men who, glomming on to Holden's estrangement, yield to the terrifying temptations of murder. "Lacking a sense of who he is," such a person "shops among artifacts of our culture—books, movies, TV programs, song lyrics, newspaper clippings—to fashion a character." Instead of authentic individuality, Priscilla Johnson McMillan has written, "all that is left is a collection of cultural shards—the bits and pieces of popular culture, torn from their contexts." [10]

In December 1980, with a copy of Salinger's novel in his pocket, Mark David Chapman murdered John Lennon. Before the police arrived, the assassin began reading the novel to himself and, when he was sentenced, read aloud the passage that begins with "anyway, I keep picturing all these little kids" and ends with "I'd just be the catcher in the rye and all" (pp. 224-25). Daniel M. Stashower has speculated ingeniously that Chapman wanted the former Beatle's innocence to be preserved in the only way possible—by death (the fate of Holden's revered brother Allie). Of course it could be argued that the assassin was not a conscientious reader, since Holden realizes on the carrousel that children have to be left alone, that they cannot be saved from themselves: "The thing with kids is, if they want to grab for the gold ring, you have to let them do it, and not say anything. If they fall off, they fall off" (pp. 273-74). No older catcher should try to intervene. [11]

Nor was Chapman the only Beatles fan to reify happiness as a warm gun. John Hinckley, Jr., described himself in his high school days as "a rebel without a cause" and was shocked to hear that Lennon had been murdered.

A year later Hinckley himself tried to kill President Reagan. In Hinckley's hotel room, police found, along with a 1981 John Lennon color calendar, Salinger's novel among a half-dozen paperbacks. Noting the "gruesome congruences between these loners," Richard Schickel wondered whether Chapman and Hinckley could "really believe their disaffections were similar to Holden Caulfield's."[12]

One stab at an answer would be provided in John Guare's play *Six Degrees of Separation*, which opened in New York in 1990 and which he adapted for Fred Schepsi's film three years later. An imposter calling himself Paul insinuates himself into a well-heeled family; he is a perfect stranger (or appears to be). Pretending to be a Harvard undergraduate who has just been mugged, posing as the son of actor Sidney Poitier, Paul claims that his thesis is devoted to Salinger's novel and its odd connections to criminal loners:

A substitute teacher out on Long Island was dropped from his job for fighting with a student. A few weeks later, the teacher returned to the classroom, shot the student unsuccessfully, held the class hostage and then shot himself successfully. This fact caught my eye: last sentence. *Times.* A neighbor described him as a nice boy. Always reading *Catcher in the Rye.*

Paul then mentions "the nitwit-Chapman" and insists that "the reading of that book would be his defense" for having killed Lennon. Hinckley, too, had "said if you want my defense all you have to do is read *Catcher in the Rye.* It seemed to be time to read it again." Paul reads it as a "manifesto of hate" against phonies, a touching story, comic because the boy wants to do so much and can't do anything. Hates all phoniness and only lies to others. Wants everyone to like him, is only hateful, and is completely self-involved. In other words, a pretty accurate picture of a male adolescent. And what alarms me about the book—not the book so much as the aura about it—is this: The book is primarily about paralysis. The boy can't function. And at the end, before he can run away and start a new life, it starts to rain and he folds. . . . But the aura around this book of Salinger's—which perhaps should be read by everyone but young men—is this: It mirrors like a fun house mirror and amplifies like a distorted speaker one of the great tragedies of our times—the death of the imagination, [which] now stands as a synonym for something outside ourselves.

A smooth liar, Paul later admits (or claims) that a Groton commencement address delivered a couple of years earlier was the source of his insights.[13]

Holden has thus been born to trouble—yet another reminder that, in the opinion of long queues of literary critics, you can't know about him without your having read a book by Mr. Mark Twain called *The Adventures of Huckleberry Finn*, which told the truth mainly about the intensity of the yearning for authenticity and innocence that marks the picaresque quest. Huck and Holden share the fate of being both beloved and banned; such reactions were not unrelated. When the Concord (Massachusetts) public library proscribed *The Adventures of Huckleberry Finn* soon after its publication, the author gloated that not even his *Innocents Abroad* had sold more copies more quickly; and "those idiots in Concord" "have given us a rattling tip-top puff which will go into every paper in the country. . . . That will sell 25,000 copies for us sure."[14]

Salinger's novel does not appear to have been kept off the shelves in Concord but did cause enough of a stir to make the short list of the most banned books in school libraries, curricula, and public libraries.[15] In 1973 the *American School Board Journal* called this monster best-seller "the most widely censored book in the United States." [16] It was noted nearly a decade later that *The Catcher in the Rye* "had the dubious distinction of being at once the most frequently censored book across the nation and the second-most frequently taught novel in public high schools." [17] Anne Levinson, the assistant director of the Office of Intellectual Freedom in Chicago, called *The Catcher in the Rye* probably "a perennial No. 1 on the censorship hit list," narrowly ahead of *Of Mice and Men* and *The Grapes of Wrath* and perhaps of Eldridge Cleaver's *Soul on Ice* as well.[18] No postwar American novel has been subjected to more—and more intense—efforts to prevent the young from reading it.

Some examples: The National Organization for Decent Literature declared it objectionable by 1956. Five years later a teacher in a San Jose, California, high school who had included the novel on the twelfth-grade supplementary reading list was transferred and the novel dropped. *The Catcher in the Rye* was excised from the list of approved books in Kershaw County, South Carolina, after the sheriff of Camden declared part of the novel obscene.[19] In 1978 the novel was banned in the high schools of Issaquah, Washington, in the wake of a campaign led by a diligent citizen who tabulated 785 "profanities" and charged that including Holden in the syllabus was "part of an overall Communist plot in which a lot of people are used and may not even be aware of it."[20] Three school board members in Issaquah not only voted in favor of banning *The Catcher in the Rye* but also against renewing the contract of the school superintendent who had explicitly sanctioned the right of English teachers to assign the book. The board members were recalled, however. A school board member also confiscated a copy of Salinger's novel from a high school library in Asheville, North Carolina, in 1973. Several high school teachers have been fired or forced to resign for having assigned *The Catcher in the Rye*.[21]

California was the site of two well-reported incidents. The first erupted in 1962 in Temple City, near Pasadena, at a Board of Education meeting. Salinger's book had been assigned as supplementary reading for the eleventh grade. A parent objected, in the main, to the "crude, profane and obscene" language. For good measure, though, the book was also condemned for its literary assault on patriotism, "home life, [the] teaching profession, religion and so forth." Another vigilant parent, imploring the President of the United States summarily to fire anyone writing such a book, had obviously confused the reclusive novelist with John F. Kennedy's amiable press secretary, Pierre Salinger.[22]

The Catcher in the Rye was also banned from the supplementary reading list of Boron High School, located on the edge of the Mojave Desert. The proscription had an interesting effect. Salinger "has gained a new readership among townspeople," the *New York Times* reported, "and Helen Nelson, the local librarian, has a waiting list of fifteen people for the book that she says has been sitting on the shelf all these years pretty much unnoticed." The campaign against the book had been fueled by its profanity, which aroused the most heated objections. Vickie Swindler, the parent of a fourteen-year-old girl, was startled to see three "goddamns" on page 32. She recalled phoning the school and demanding to know: "How the hell [sic] did this teacher [Shelley Keller-Gage] get this book?" Locals who sympathized with the censors offered a curious interpretation of their motives, which they compared to Holden's dream of becoming a catcher in the rye to keep innocence intact; the protagonist and the parents trying to muzzle him shared a desire to exempt children from the vulgarity and corruption of the adult world. Yet, as Mrs. Keller-Gage noted, "Things are not innocent any more, and I think we've got to help them [i.e., children] deal with that, to make responsible choices, to be responsible citizens." Parents were "wanting to preserve the innocence of the children" in vain. The *Times* reported that she offered an alternative assignment for pupils whose parents were opposed to *The Catcher in the Rye*: Ray Bradbury's *Dandelion Wine*.[23]

When the ban took effect in the new term, Mrs. Keller-Gage put her three-dozen copies of Salinger's novel "on a top shelf of her classroom closet, inside a tightly taped cardboard box." Raise high the bookshelf, censors. In place of *The Catcher in the Rye*, she announced, she would assign another Bradbury novel, *Fahrenheit 451*,[24] the title referring to the presumed "temperature at which book-paper catches fire, and burns." This dystopian novel about book-burning was published in 1953, though a shorter version, entitled "The Fireman," had appeared in *Galaxy Science Fiction* in 1950. Both versions were too early to allude to Salinger's novel, which is neither shown nor recited in Francois Truffaut's 1966 film adaptation (though one item visibly consumed is an issue of *Cahiers du Cinema*).

Efforts at suppression were not confined to secondary schools. A prominent Houston attorney, "whose daughter had been assigned the novel in an English class at the University of Texas, threatened to remove the girl from the University," *Harper's* reported. "The aggrieved father sent copies [of the novel] to the governor, the chancellor of the university, and a number of state officials. The state senator from Houston threatened to read passages from the book on the senate floor to show the sort of thing they teach in Austin. The lawyer-father said Salinger used language `no sane person would use' and accused the university of `corrupting the moral fibers [sic] of our youth.'" He conceded that the novel "is not a hard-core Communist-type book, but it encourages a lessening of spiritual values which in turn leads to communism."[25]

In making appointments to the department of English at the University of Montana, Leslie A. Fiedler recalled that "the only unforgivable thing in the university or the state was to be `controversial.'" He nevertheless "began to make offers to young instructors who had quarreled with their administrators, or had asked their students to read *Catcher in the Rye*, or had themselves written poetry containing dirty words, or were flagrantly Jewish or simply Black." The narrator of a recent academic novel, *Mustang Sally*, recalls that "the chairman of the department has asked us all to use our best judgment in avoiding confrontation with the evangelicals . . . such as the group who staged a pray-in at the Greensburg High School library because *The Catcher in the Rye* was on the shelves. It has since been removed, along with the principal." No wonder, then, that one columnist, though writing for the newspaper of record, whimsically claimed to "lose count of the number of times the book has been challenged or banned."[26]

Such animosity had become a predictable feature of the far right by the 1980s, when an outfit named Educational Research Analysts, financed by Richard Viguerie, a leading fundraiser for right-wing organizations, was formed to examine nearly every textbook considered for adoption anywhere in the nation. "The group has assembled a list of 67 categories under which a book may be banned. Category 43 ('Trash') included *The Catcher in the Rye*," the *New Republic* reported. Perhaps Salinger should have counted his blessings, since the eclectic Category 44 consisted of the "works of questionable writers" like Malcolm X, Langston Hughes, and Ogden Nash.[27]

It is more surprising that moral objections surfaced in the pages of *Ramparts*, the brashest of the magazines to give a radical tincture to the 1960s. The monthly had begun under Roman Catholic auspices, however; and though Simone de Beauvoir's *The Second Sex* was deemed a work of depravity on the Index Librorum Prohibitorum, Salinger was accorded the same treatment as Genet, Proust, Joyce, and D. H. Lawrence: omission.[28] But individual Catholics could still get incensed over *The Catcher in the Rye*, as the new editor of *Ramparts*, Warren Hinckle, discovered one evening. He was having a conversation with the new fiction editor, Helen Keating, who was married to the magazine's new publisher. Hinckle recalled: A great debate somehow began over the rather precious subject of J.D. Salinger. The setting was vaguely Inquisitional. . . . They all listened attentively as [Edward] Keating, suddenly a fiery prosecutor, denounced Salinger for moral turpitude. Keating expressed similar opinions about the degeneracy of writers such as Tennessee Williams and Henry Miller: corruption, moral decay, the erosion of the classic values of Western Civilization, et cetera, ad infinitum. His special contempt for Salinger seemed to have something to do with the fact that he had found his oldest son reading a paperback book by the man.

Keating became enraged enough to make "the hyperbolic assertion, which he later retracted, that if he were President, he would put J.D. Salinger in jail! I asked why. `Because he's dirty,' Ed said. I barely recalled something in *The Catcher in the Rye* about Holden Caulfield in the back seat unhooking a girl's bra," Hinckle recalled. Despite the lyric, "If a body catch a body," in fact few popular novels are so fully exempt from the leer of the sensualist; and even though Holden claims to be "probably the biggest sex maniac you ever saw," he admits it's only "in my mind" (p. 81).

In any case, Hinckle was baffled by Keating's tirade and "unleashed a more impassioned defense of Salinger than I normally would have felt impelled to make of a voguish writer whose mortal sin was his Ivy League slickness." The chief consequence of the argument was Keating's discovery of a "bomb," by which he meant "a hot story. The 'bomb' which exploded in the first issue of *Ramparts* was the idea of a symposium on J.D. Salinger"— with Hinckle for the defense and Keating and a friend of his for the prosecution. That friend, Robert O. Bowen, complained in the inaugural issue in 1962 that Salinger was not only anti-Catholic but somehow also "pro-Jewish and proNegro." Bowen accused the novelist of being so subversive that he was "vehemently anti-Army" (though Salinger had landed on Utah Beach on D-Day), "even anti-America," a writer who subscribed to "the sick line transmitted by Mort Sahl" and other "cosmopolitan think people." Though Bowen was vague in identifying the sinister campaigns this impenetrably private novelist was managing to wage, alignments with the AntiDefamation League and "other Jewish pressure groups" were duly noted, and Salinger's sympathy for "Negro chauvinism" was denounced. "Let those of us who are Christian and who love life lay this book aside as the weapon of an enemy," Bowen advised.[29] Such was the level of literary analysis at the birth of *Ramparts*.

The Catcher in the Rye has even taken on an iconic significance precisely because it is reviled as well as revered. What if the Third Reich had won the Second World War by defeating Britain? one novelist has wondered. Set in 1964, *Fatherland* imagines a past in which Salinger is among four foreign authors listed as objectionable to the Greater Reich. Those writers, banned by the authorities, are esteemed by younger Germans "rebelling against their parents. Questioning the state. Listening to American radio stations. Circulating their crudely printed copies of proscribed books. . . . Chiefly, they protested against the war—the seemingly endless struggle against the American-backed Soviet guerrillas." But forget about a history that never happened. One of the two regimes that had supplanted the defeated Reich was the German Democratic Republic, whose censors were wary of American cultural imports. In the 1960s, Kurt Hager served as the leading ideologist on the Central Committee of the East German regime. Resisting publication of a translation of Salinger's novel, Hager feared that its protagonist might captivate Communist youth. Though a translation did eventually appear and proved popular among young readers in the GDR, Hager refused to give up the fight. Appropriate role models were "winners," he insisted, like the regime's Olympic athletes, not "losers" like Holden Caulfield.[30]

Yet anti-anti-Communism could make use of the novel too. Its reputation for inciting censorious anxiety had become so great by 1990 that in the film *Guilty by Suspicion*, a terrified screenwriter is shown burning his books in his driveway a few hours after testifying before a rump session of the House UnAmerican Activities Committee. Shocked at this bonfire of the humanities, director David Merrill (Robert De Niro) categorizes what goes up in flames as "all good books"—though the only titles he cites are *The Adventures of Tom Sawyer* and *The Catcher in the Rye*. The decision of writer-director Irwin Winkler to include Salinger's novel, however, is historically (if not canonically) implausible. When the film opens in September 1951, Merrill is shown returning from two months in France; a hot-off-the-press copy of the best-seller must therefore have been rushed to him in Paris if he could pronounce on the merits of the book on his first evening back in Los Angeles.

The attacks on *The Catcher in the Rye* gathered a momentum of their own and "show no signs of tapering off," one student of book banning concluded in 1979. The novel became so notorious for igniting controversy "that many censors freely admit they have never read it, but are relying on the reputation the book has garnered."[31] Anne Levinson added: "Usually the complaints have to do with blasphemy or what people feel is irreligious. Or they say they find the language generally offensive or vulgar, or there is a sort of general 'family values' kind of complaint, that the book undermines parental authority, that the portrayal of Holden Caulfield is not a good role model for teenagers." It was judged suitable for Chelsea Clinton, however. In 1993 the First Lady gave her daughter a copy to read while vacationing on Martha's Vineyard. The *Boston Globe* used the occasion to editorialize against persistent censorship, since "Salinger's novel of a 1950s coming of age still ranks among the works most frequently challenged by parents seeking to sanitize their children's school reading."[32]

Assigning Meaning to Growing Up Absurd

Few American novels of the postwar era have elicited as much scholarly and critical attention as *The Catcher in the Rye*, and therefore little that is fresh can still be proposed about so closely analyzed a text. But the social context within which the novel has generated such anxiety remains open to interpretation. If anything new can be said about this book, its status within the cross-hairs of censors offers the greatest promise. What needs further consideration is not why this novel is so endearing but why it has inspired campaigns to ban it. Literary critics have tended to expose the uncanny artistry by which Salinger made Holden Caulfield into the loved one but have been far less curious about the intensity of the desire to muffle him. It is nevertheless possible to isolate several explanations for the power of this novel to affect—and disturb—readers outside of departments of English.

The "culture wars" of the last third of the twentieth century are fundamentally debates about the 1960s. That decade marked the end of what historian Tom Engelhardt has labeled "victory culture," indeed the end of "the American Way of Life," phrased in the singular. The 1960s constituted a caesura in the formation of national self-definition, nor has confidence in *e pluribus unum* been entirely restored. At first glance it might seem surprising for *The Catcher in the Rye* to have contributed in some small fashion to fragmentation. Nevertheless such a case, however tentative, has been advanced. Since nothing in history is created *ex nihilo*, at least part of the 1960s, it has been argued, must have sprung from at least part of the 1950s. Literary critics Carol and Richard Ohmann, for example, concede that the young narrator lacks the will to try to change society. They nevertheless contend that his creator recorded "a serious critical mimesis of bourgeois life in the Eastern United States, ca. 1950—of snobbery, privilege, class injury, culture as a badge of superiority, sexual exploitation, education subordinated to status, warped social feeling, competitiveness, stunted human possibility, the list could go on." They praise Salinger's acuity "in imagining these hurtful things, though not in explaining them"—or in hinting how they might be corrected. *The Catcher in the Rye* thus "mirrors a contradiction of bourgeois society" and of "advanced capitalism," which promises many good things but frustrates their acquisition and equitable distribution. In this manner readers are encouraged at least to conceive of the urgent need for change, even if they're not able to reconfigure Holden's musings into a manual for enacting it.[33]

That moment would have to await the crisis of the Vietnam War, which "converted Salinger's novel into a catalyst for revolt, converting anomie into objectified anger," John Seelye has argued. *The Catcher in the Rye* became "a threshold text to the decade of the sixties, ten years after it appeared at the start of the fifties, [when it was] a minority text stating a minor view." In the axial shift to the left that occurred in the 1960s, the sensibility of a prep school drop-out could be re-charged and politicized: "*Catcher* likewise supplied not only the rationale for the antiwar, anti-regimentation movements of the sixties and seventies but provided the anti-ideological basis for many of the actual novels about Vietnam."[34]

The 1960s mavericks ("the highly sensitive, the tormented") who would brand social injustice as itself obscene were, according to Charles Reich, real-life versions of what Holden had groped toward becoming. Salinger's protagonist may be too young, or too rich, to bestir himself outward. But he was "a fictional version of the first young precursors of Consciousness III. Perhaps there was always a bit of Consciousness III in every teenager, but normally it quickly vanished. Holden sees through the established world: they are phonies and he is merciless in his honesty. But what was someone like Holden to do? A subculture of 'beats' grew up, and a beatnik world flourished briefly, but for most people it represented only another dead end," Reich commented. "Other Holdens might reject the legal profession and try teaching literature or writing instead, letting their hair grow a little bit longer as well. But they remained separated individuals, usually ones from affluent but unhappy, tortured family backgrounds, and their differences with society were paid for by isolation." In making America more green, Holden was portrayed as an avatar of "subterranean awareness."[35]

Daniel Isaacson also reads the novel as seeding later revolt. The narrator of E. L. Doctorow's *The Book of Daniel*, published exactly two decades after *The Catcher in the Rye*, even echoes Holden in self-consciously repudiating Dickens's contribution to Con II: "Let's see, what other David Copperfield kind of crap" should he tell you? But the personal quickly becomes political, when Daniel insists that "the Trustees of Ohio State were right in 1956 when they canned the English instructor for assigning *Catcher in the Rye* to his freshman class. They knew there is no qualitative difference between the kid who thinks it's funny to fart in chapel, and Che Guevara. They knew then Holden Caulfield would found SDS."[36]

Of course Daniel thinks of himself as an outcast and is eager to re-establish and legitimate his radical lineage, and so his assumption that the trustees might have been shrewd enough to foresee guerrillas in the mist must be treated with skepticism. But consider Tom Hayden, a founder of Students for a Democratic Society (and in the 1950s a parishioner of Father Charles Coughlin in Royal Oak, Michigan). As a teenager Hayden had considered Salinger's protagonist (along with novelist Jack Kerouac and actor James Dean) an "alternative cultural model." "The life crises they personified spawned. . . political activism," which some who had been adolescents in the 1950s found liberating. Hayden remembers being touched not only by Holden's assault on the "phonies" and conformists but by his "caring side," his sympathy for "underdogs and innocents." The very "attempt to be gentle and humane . . . makes Holden a loser in the 'game' of life. Unable to be the kind of man required by prep schools and corporations," Salinger's protagonist could find no exit within American society. Undefiant and confused, Holden nevertheless served as "the first image of middle-class youth growing up absurd," which Hayden would situate at the psychological center of the Port Huron Statement.[37]

The dynamism inherent in youthful revolt, one historian has claimed, can best be defined as "a mystique . . . that fused elements of Marlon Brando's role in *The Wild One*, James Dean's portrayal in *Rebel without a Cause*, J.D. Salinger's Holden Caulfield in *Catcher in the Rye*, the rebels of *Blackboard Jungle*, and the driving energy and aggressive sexuality of the new heroes of rock 'n' roll into a single image. The mystique emphasized a hunger for authenticity and sensitivity." But something is askew here, for Holden is too young to have felt the Dionysian effects of rock 'n' roll, which erupted about three years after he left Pencey Prep. A "sex maniac" only in his head, he hardly represents "aggressive sexuality" either. *The Wild One*, *Rebel without a Cause*, and *Blackboard Jungle* are "goddam movies," which Holden professes to hate, because "they can ruin you. I'm not kidding" (p. 136). His own tastes are emphatically literary, ranging from *The Great Gatsby* and *Out of Africa* to *Thomas Hardy* and *Ring Lardner*. Even if the bland official ethos of the 1950s ultimately failed to repress the rambunctious energies the popular arts were about to unleash, Roland Marchand understands that the "mystique" he has identified would not be easily radicalized. Indeed, it could be tamed. Conservative consolidation was a more predictable outcome: "If the problems of a society are embedded in its social structure and are insulated from change by layers of ideological tradition, popular culture is an unlikely source of remedy. It is far more likely to serve needs for diversion and transitory compensation . . . [and] solace."[38] Such dynamism could not be politicized.

The deeper flaw with interpreting *The Catcher in the Rye* as a harbinger of revolt is the aura of passivity that pervades the novel. Alienation does not always lead to, and can remain the antonym of, action. Salinger's own sensibility was definitively pre- (or anti-) Sixties. His "conviction that our inner lives greatly matter," John Updike observed in 1961, "peculiarly qualifies him to sing of an America, where, for most of us, there seems little to do but to feel. Introversion, perhaps, has been forced upon history" rather than the other way around. Therefore "an age of nuance, of ambiguous gestures and psychological jockeying" could account for the popularity of Salinger's work.[39]

Describing Holden as "a misfit in society because he refuses to adjust" and because he lacks the self-discipline to cultivate privacy, one young literary critic of the fifties was struck by "the quixotic futility" of the protagonist's "outrage" at all the planet's obscenities, by his isolation. Holden seems to have sat for psychologist Kenneth Keniston's portrait of uncommitted youth: those who have the most to live for but find no one to look up to; those who are the most economically and socially advantaged but feel the deepest pangs of alienation.[40] Jack Newfield ('60) was a charter member of SDS but remembers Hunter College as mired in an apathy "no public question seemed to touch." His fellow students "were bereft of passions, of dreams, of gods. . . . And their Zeitgeist—J.D. Salinger—stood for a total withdrawal from reality into the womb of childhood, innocence, and mystical Zen." Holden's creator, evidently, had captured the spirit of the Silent Generation.[41]

It may not be accidental that David Riesman, whose most famous book was a veritable touchstone of social analysis in the era, assigned *The Catcher in the Rye* in his Harvard sociology course on Character and Social Structure in the United States. He did so "perhaps," a *Time* reporter speculated, "because every campus has its lonely crowd of imitation Holdens." Indeed, Holden demonstrates the characteristics of anomie, which is associated with "ruleless" and "ungoverned" conduct, that Riesman had described in *The Lonely Crowd*; the anomic are "virtually synonymous with [the] maladjusted." Though Salinger's narrator does not quite exhibit "the lack of emotion and emptiness of expression" by which "the ambulatory patients of modern culture" can be recognized, he does display a "vehement hatred of institutional confines" that was bound to make his peers (if not his psychoanalyst) uneasy.[42] One reviewer, in true Fifties fashion, even blamed Holden himself for his loneliness, "because he has shut himself away from the normal activities of boyhood, games, the outdoors, friendship."[43] It is true that Holden hates schools like Pencey Prep, where "you have to keep making believe you give a damn if the football team loses, and all you do is talk about girls and liquor and sex all day, and everybody sticks together in these dirty little goddam cliques" (p. 170). But Holden remains confined to his era, unable to connect the dots from those cliques to a larger society that might merit some rearrangement. Nor does the novel expand the reader's horizons beyond those of the narrator; it does not get from pathos to indignation.

For *The Catcher in the Rye* is utterly apolitical—unlike its only rival in arousing the ire of conservative parents. Steinbeck's fiction directs the attention of susceptible young readers to exploitation of the weak and the abuse of power. But a serious critique of capitalism would not be found in Salinger's text even if a full field investigation were ordered. Certainly Holden's fantasy of secluding himself in a cabin in the woods is scarcely a prescription for social activism: "I'd pretend I was one of those deaf-mutes. That way I wouldn't have to have any goddam stupid useless conversations with anybody. If anybody wanted to tell me something, they'd have to write it on a piece of paper and shove it over to me. They'd get bored as hell doing that after a while, and then I'd be through with having conversations for the rest of my life" (pp. 257-58). Such passages will hardly alarm those wishing to repudiate or erase the 1960s, which is why *The Catcher in the Rye* does not belong to the history of dissidence.

Growing Up Absurd (1960) sports a title and a perspective that Holden might have appreciated, but Paul Goodman does not mention the novel. Published at the end of the tumultuous, unpredictable decade, Theodore Roszak's *The Making of a Counter Culture* (which *Newsweek* dubbed "the best guide yet published to the meaning. . . of youthful dissent") likewise fails to mention Salinger, though Holden certainly personifies (or anticipates) "the ethos of disaffiliation that is fiercely obnoxious to the adult society." In 1962 the editor of a collection of critical essays on Salinger—the future editor-in-chief of *Time*—found American campuses innocent of activism: "'Student riots' are a familiar and significant factor in European politics. The phenomenon has no equivalent in the United States."[44] That generalization would soon be falsified. But it should be noted that authors who have fathomed how the 1950s became the 1960s (like Morris Dickstein, Fred Inglis, Maurice Isserman, James Miller) ignore the impact of Salinger's novel.

Because any reading of the novel as a prefiguration of the 1960s is ultimately so unpersuasive, an over-reaction has set in. Alan Nadel, for example, has fashioned Holden into a Cold Warrior, junior division.

"Donning his red hunting hat, he attempts to become the good Red-hunter, ferreting out the phonies and the subversives, but in so doing he emulates the bad Red-hunters," Nadel has written. "Uncovering duplicity was the theme of the day," he adds, so that "in thinking constantly about who or what was phony, Caulfield was doing no more than following the instructions of J. Edgar Hoover, the California Board of Regents, The Nation [sic], the Smith Act, and the Hollywood Ten. . . . Each citizen was potentially both the threat and the threatened." After all, hadn't Gary Cooper, testifying before HUAC, defined Communism as something that was not "on the level"? Nadel equates Caulfield's "disdain for Hollywood" with HUAC's, nor could the young prostitute's mention of Melvyn Douglas have been accidental—since Congressman Richard Nixon had run against Helen Gahagan Douglas, and her husband was himself "a prominent Hollywood liberal." Nadel concludes that "the solution to Caulfield's dilemma becomes renouncing speech itself." Having named names, he realizes: "I sort of miss everybody I told about. . . . It's funny. Don't ever tell anybody anything," he advises; that is, don't be an informer. "If you do, you start missing everybody" (pp. 276-77). The narrator "spoke for the cold war HUAC witness," Nadel argued, "expressing existential angst over the nature and meaning of his `testimony.'"[45] Such an interpretation is far-fetched: Holden is no more interested in politics than his creator, and he's considerably less interested in sanctioning conformity than were the Red-hunters.

Citizens who abhor the 1960s commonly deplore one of its most prominent legacies: the fragmentation into "identity politics," the loss of civic cohesion. Those worrying over this sin also will not find it in Salinger's book, which promotes no class consciousness, racial consciousness, or ethnic consciousness of any sort. Sol Salinger had strayed so far from Judaism that he became an importer of hams and cheeses;[46] and his son left no recognizably Jewish imprint on his fiction. Nor does his novel evoke the special plight of young women and girls. That omission would be rectified about two generations later, when Eve Horowitz's first novel appeared. Her young narrator and protagonist is not only female but emphatically Jewish, and she longs to meet her own Holden Caulfield. Jane Singer recalls: "I hadn't known any males who were as depressed as I was in high school, except for maybe Holden Caulfield, and I didn't really know him." As she's packing to leave Cleveland for Oberlin College, she muses, "besides clothes and shampoo and *The Catcher in the Rye*, I couldn't think of anything else to bring."[47] In her account of growing up female, Horowitz may have wanted to correct the imbalance David Riesman identified in 1961, when, attempting to explain the United States to a Japanese audience, he had commented on the inscrutable popularity of Salinger's novel: "Boys are frustrated because they aren't cowboys, and girls are frustrated because they aren't boys." The sociologist noted that "women have been the audience for American fiction and for movies. There are no girls' stories comparable to *Catcher in the Rye*. Yet girls can adapt themselves and identify with such a book, while a boy can't so easily identify with a girl."[48] In the literary marketplace, Riesman speculated, readers aren't turned off or away if the central characters are male but only if they are female. How many Boy Scouts and Explorer Scouts have been moved by reading *The Bell Jar*?

THE CURSE OF CULTURE

Another way to understand the power of Salinger's novel to generate controversy is to recognize its vulnerability to moralistic criticism. From wherever the source—call it Puritanism, or puritanism, or Victorianism—there persists a tradition of imposing religious standards upon art or of rejecting works of the imagination because they violate conventional ethical codes. According to this legacy, books are neither good nor bad without "for you" being added as a criterion of judgment. This entwining of the aesthetic and the moralistic was obvious as prize committees struggled with the terms of Joseph Pulitzer's instructions that the novels to be honored in his name "shall best present the whole atmosphere of American life." But until 1927, the novels selected more accurately conveyed "the wholesome atmosphere of American life."[49] That eliminated Dreiser. Had the subtle revision of Pulitzer's own intentions not been overturned, virtually all great writers would have been categorically excluded. Nabokov comes quickly to mind. His most famous novel was given to the good family man Adolf Eichmann, then imprisoned in Israel, but was returned after two days with an indignant rejection: "Das ist aber ein sehr unerfreuliches Buch"—quite an unwholesome book. *Lolita* is narrated from the viewpoint of an adult, a pervert whose ornate vocabulary made the novel unintelligible to young readers, and so censors passed it by to target *The Catcher in the Rye*. It is a measure of Salinger's stature among other writers that, though famously dismissive of many literary giants, Nabokov wrote privately of his fellow *New Yorker* contributor: "I do admire him very much."[50]

But the reviewer for *The Christian Science Monitor* did not: *The Catcher in the Rye* "is not fit for children to read"; its central character is "preposterous, profane, and pathetic beyond belief." Too many young readers might even want to emulate Holden, "as too easily happens when immorality and perversion are recounted by writers of talent whose work is countenanced in the name of art or good intention."[51] Here was an early sign of trouble. Nor was respectability enhanced by the novel's first appearance in paperback, for it was offered as pulp fiction, a genre that beckoned with promises of illicit pleasure. The common 1950s practice of issuing serious books in pulp meant that "dozens of classic novels appeared in packages that were cartoonish, sordid or merely absurd." The aim of such marketing, Julie Lasky has suggested, was to grab "the attention of impulse shoppers in drugstores and bus depots; slogans jammed across the four-inch width of paperbound covers compressed the nuances of prizewinning authors into exaggerated come-ons." The 1953 paperback edition of Salinger's novel, for example, assured buyers that "this unusual book may shock you . . . but you will never forget it." The illustration on the cover depicted a prostitute standing near Holden and may have served as the only means by which some citizens judged the book. The cover so offended the author that it contributed to his move to Bantam when his contract with Signet expired. By then, the pulping of classics had largely ended in the wake of hearings by the House of Representatives Select Committee on Current Pornographic Materials. But the availability of such cheap editions of books ranging from the serious to the lurid drew the curiosity of censors as well as bargain-hunters. The vulnerability of Salinger's novel testified to the aptness of Walter Lippmann's generalization that censorship "is actually applied in proportion to the vividness, the directness, and the intelligibility of the medium which circulates the subversive idea." Movie screens, he wrote in 1927, therefore tend to be more censored than the stage, which is more censored than newspapers and magazines. But "the novel is even freer than the press today because it is an even denser medium of expression."[52] At least that was the case until the paperback revolution facilitated the expansion of the syllabus.

Of course, the paperback revolution was not the only cultural shift affecting the reception of the novel. The career of *The Catcher in the Rye* is virtually synchronous with the Cold War, and Holden Caulfield takes a stand of sorts: he calls himself "a pacifist" (p. 59). For men slightly older than Holden in 1949-50, military conscription was more or less universal, yet he predicts that "it'd drive me crazy if I had to be in the Army. . . . I swear if there's ever another war, they better just take me out and stick me in front of a firing squad. I wouldn't object." Indeed he goes further: "I'm sort of glad they've got the atomic bomb invented. If there's ever another war, I'm going to sit right the hell on top of it. I'll volunteer for it, I swear to God I will" (pp. 182, 183). Barely a decade later, Stanley Kubrick's pitch-black comedy *Dr. Strangelove* (1964) would confront nuclear terror by showing Major "King" Kong (Slim Pickens) doing precisely what Holden vows he will step forward to do. With such images in mind, one interpreter has thus boldly claimed that "the fear of nuclear holocaust, not the fear of four-letter words[,]" sparked controversy about *The Catcher in the Rye*.[53]

Salinger's novel may thus also be about history veering out of control, about the abyss into which parents could no longer prevent their offspring from staring, about the impotence to which a can-do people was unaccustomed. "The lack of faith in the American character expressed in the *Catcher* controversies," Professor Pamela Steinle has argued, "is rooted not in doubts about the strength of adolescent Americans' character but in recognition of the powerlessness of American adults—as parents, professionals and community leaders—to provide a genuine sense of the future for the adolescents in their charge." According to Steinle, the novel indicts "adult apathy and complicity in the construction of a social reality in which the American character cannot develop in any meaningful sense beyond adolescence." Nor does the novel warrant any hope that the condition can be remedied. The story is, after all, told from a sanitarium in California—a grim terminus given the common belief that the West offers a second chance. No wonder, then, that John Seelye, who ended his own revised version of *The Adventures of Huckleberry Finn* with Huck's bleakest pessimism ("I didn't much care if the goddamn sun never come up again"), could read Salinger's book "as a lengthy suicide note with a blank space at the end to sign your name."[54]

The advantage of Steinle's argument is that she situates the controversy over *The Catcher in the Rye* where it actually took place, which is less in the pages of *Ramparts* than at school board meetings. In such settings, the novel was branded by parents as a threat to their control and heralded by teachers as a measure of their professional autonomy and authority. But the disadvantage of Steinle's view is the scarcity of direct evidence that nuclear fears fueled the debate. Neither those who condemned *The Catcher in the Rye* nor its defenders made the specter of atomic catastrophe pivotal. Neither the moral nor the literary disputes were ventilated in such terms. Compared to Holden's far more pronounced resistance to maturation, compared to more immediate targets of his scorn, the Bomb hardly registered as a concern among objections to the novel.

But if "the essence of censorship," according to Lippmann, is "not to suppress subversive ideas as such, but to withhold them from those who are young or unprivileged or otherwise undependable,"[55] then Steinle's emphasis upon parental assertion of authority is not misplaced. In a more class-conscious society, the Old Bailey prosecutor of the publisher of *Lady Chatterley's Lover* could ask in his opening address to the jury, in 1960: "Is it a book that you would even wish your wife or your servants to read?"[56] But in the United States, overt conflicts are more likely to take generational form; and the first of Lippmann's categories deserves to be highlighted. Some of the books that have aroused the greatest ire place children at the center, like Richard Wright's *Black Boy*, Anne Frank's *Diary of a Young Girl*, and of course *The Adventures of Huckleberry Finn*; and despite the aura of "cuteness" hovering over Salinger's work, it emitted danger by striking at the most vulnerable spot in the hearts of parents. Nor could it have escaped the attention of alert readers that Holden's emotional affiliations are horizontal rather than vertical. His father, a corporate lawyer, is absent from the scene; and his mother is present only as a voice speaking from a dark room. The only relative whom the reader meets is Phoebe, the younger sister (and a mini-Holden).[57]

The contributor's note Salinger submitted to *Harper's* in 1946 was his credo: "I almost always write about very young people";[58] and the directness with which he spoke to them had much to do with his appeal—and with the anxiety that his literary intervention provoked in the internecine battle between generations. The effectiveness of his empathy posed a challenge to parents who invoked their right to be custodians of the curriculum, and the "legions of decency" may have sensed "a unique seductive power" which Salinger's biographer claims *The Catcher in the Rye* exudes. Even if the less sensitive or eccentric of its young readers might not try to assume Holden's persona, at least teenagers could imitate his lingo. A book that elicits such proprietary interest—succeeding cohorts believing in a special access to Salinger's meaning—was bound to arouse some suspicion that conventional authority was being outflanked.[59] Salinger's adroit fidelity to the feelings and experiences of his protagonist was what made the novel so tempting a target. Perhaps *The Catcher in the Rye* has been banned precisely because it is so cherished; because it is so easily loved, some citizens love to hate it.

Steinle has closely examined the local controversies that erupted over the book in Alabama, Virginia, New Mexico, and California as well as the debates conducted in such publications as the *PTA Magazine* and the *Newsletter on Intellectual Freedom* of the American Library Association. She discovered a "division . . . over whether to prepare adolescents for or to protect them from adult disillusionment. . . . In the postwar period . . . recognition of the increasing dissonance between American ideals and the realities of social experience has become unavoidable, and it is precisely this cultural dissonance that is highlighted by Salinger's novel."[60] Its literary value got lost in the assertion of family values, in a campaign that must be classified as reactionary. "They say it describes reality," a parent in Boron, California, announced. "I say let's back up from reality. Let's go backwards. Let's go back to when we didn't have an immoral society."[61] When so idyllic a state existed was not specified, but what is evident is the element of anti-intellectualism that the struggle against permissiveness entailed. Here some of the parents were joined by Leonard Hall, the school superintendent of Bay County, Florida, who warned in 1987 against assigning books that were not state-approved because, he sagely opined, reading "is where you get ideas from."[62]

Attempts at vindication were occasionally made on the same playing field that censors themselves chose. Though Holden labels himself "sort of an atheist" (p.130), he could be praised as a saint, if admittedly a picaresque one. One educator discerned in the protagonist a diamond in the rough: "He befriends the friendless. He respects those who are humble, loyal, and kind. He demonstrates a strong love for his family" (or for Phoebe anyway). Besides enacting such New Testament teachings, "he abhors hypocrisy. He values sex that comes from caring for another person and rejects its sordidness. And, finally, he wants to be a responsible member of society, to guide and protect those younger than he."[63] But a character witness is not the same as a literary critic, and such conflation seems to have gained little traction when the right of English teachers to make up reading lists was contested. If Holden's defense rested on a sanitized version of his character, then the implication was that assigned books with less morally meritorious protagonists might be subject to parental veto. Such a defense also assumed that disgruntled parents were themselves exegetes who had simply misread a text, that community conflicts could be resolved by more subtle interpretations. There is no reason to believe, however, that the towns where the novel was banned or challenged overlapped with maps of misreading. But such communities were places where parents tried to gain control of the curriculum, which is why *The Catcher in the Rye* would still have been proscribed even had it been re-read as a book of virtues.

For the objections that were most frequently raised were directed at the novelist's apparent desire to capture profuse adolescent profanity in the worst way. In the *Catholic World*, reviewer Riley Hughes disliked the narrator's "excessive use of amateur swearing and coarse language," which made his character simply "monotonous."[64] According to one angry parent's tabulation, 237 instances of "goddamn," 58 uses of the synonym for a person of illegitimate birth, 31 "Chrissakes," and one incident of flatulence constituted what was wrong with Salinger's book. Though blasphemy is not a crime, *The Catcher in the Rye* "uses the Lord's name in vain two hundred times," an opponent in Boron asserted—"enough [times] to ban it right there."[65] The statistics are admittedly not consistent. But it is incontestable that the text contains six examples of "fuck" or "fuck you," though here Holden is actually allied with the censorious parents, since he does not swear with this four-letter word himself but instead tries to efface it from walls. He's indignant that children should be subjected to such graffiti. Upon seeing the word even in the Egyptian tomb room at the Metropolitan Museum of Art, however, Holden achieves a melancholy and mature insight that such offenses to dignity cannot really be expunged from the world: "You can't ever find a place that's nice and peaceful, because there isn't any" (p. 264).[66]

What happened to *The Catcher in the Rye* wasn't always nice and peaceful because it took a linguistic turn. Though historians are fond of defining virtually every era as one of transition, it does make sense to locate the publication of Salinger's novel on the cusp of change. The novel benefited from the loosening of tongues that the Second World War sanctioned, yet the profanity in which Holden indulges still looked conspicuous before the 1960s. Salinger thus helped to accelerate the trend toward greater freedom for writers but found himself the target of those offended by the adolescent vernacular still rarely enough recorded in print. During the Second World War, the Production Code had been slightly relaxed for *We Are the Marines*. This 1943 March of Time documentary was permitted to use mild expletives like "damn" "under stress of battle conditions." Professor Thomas Doherty adds that, "in the most ridiculed example of the Code's tender ears, Noel Coward's *In Which We Serve* (1942), a British import, was held up from American release for seventeen words: ten 'damns,' two 'hells,' two 'Gods,' two 'bastards,' and one 'lousy.'"

Only three years before publication of Salinger's novel, homophonic language was inserted into Norman Mailer's *The Naked and the Dead* at the suggestion of his cousin, Charles Rembar. A crackerjack First Amendment attorney who would later represent such clients as Fanny Hill and Constance Chatterley, Rembar proposed the substitution of fug (as in "Fug you. Fug the goddam gun") partly because the president of the house publishing the novel feared his own mother's reaction. The U.S. Information Agency was nevertheless unpersuaded and banned Mailer's book from its overseas libraries. As late as 1952, the revised edition of *Webster's Unabridged* offered a simple but opaque definition of masturbation as "onanism; selfpollution."[67] The next year President Eisenhower delivered a celebrated plea at Dartmouth College: "Don't join the bookburners. . . . Don't be afraid to go into your library and read every book." His amendment is less cited—"as long as that document does not offend our own ideas of decency." Though the war in which Mailer and Salinger fought allowed some indecorous terms to go public, the 1960 Presidential debates included the spectacle of Nixon seeking to trump another ex-sailor by promising the electorate—after Harry Truman's salty lapsesto continue Ike's restoration of "decency and, frankly, good language" in the White House.[68]

In this particular war of words, Salinger was conscripted into a cause for which he was no more suited than any other. If he was affiliated with any institution at all, it was the *New Yorker*, which initially published most of his *Nine Stories* as well as the substance of his two subsequent books. In that magazine even the mildest profanity was strictly forbidden, and editorial prudishness would have spiked publication of excerpts from the final version of what became his most admired work. It may be plausible, as one scholar circling the text has noted, that "the radical nature of Salinger's portrayal of disappointment with American society, so much like Twain's in *Huck Finn*, was probably as much of the reason that *Catcher* (like *Huck*) was banned from schools and colleges as were the few curse words around which the battle was publicly fought."[69] But such ideological objections to Salinger's novel were rarely raised, much less articulated with any cogency; and therefore no historian of the reception of this book should minimize the salience of those "few curse words."

Could *The Catcher in the Rye* have avoided the turbulent pool into which it was so often sucked? Could the novel have been rescued from primitive detractors and retained an even more secure status in the public school curriculum? One compromise was never considered. It is the solution that Noah Webster commonly applied to dictionaries and spelling books, that Emerson recommended to Whitman for *Leaves of Grass*, and that Lewis Carroll intended to enact with a volume entitled The Girl's Own Shakespeare: expurgation. Had Holden's lingo been sanitized in accordance with the legacy of Dr. Thomas Bowdler, the moral (or moralistic) resistance to Salinger's novel would have evaporated. Bowdlerization constitutes what its leading student has called "literary slum clearance," but it also cordons off the censors. Of course Holden would not have been Holden with expletives deleted. The guileless integrity of his language makes him so memorable and therefore the novel so distinctive. Richard Watson Gilder had inflicted the kindest cuts of all on Huck's talk,[70] but by the 1950s no expurgators survived to spare Holden from the animosity he incurred. Such an explanation may be too obvious and all, if you really want to know. It's so simple it kills me, for Chrissake. But I really believe it's the best explanation. I really do.

NOTES

The author appreciates the invitation of Professors Marc Lee Raphael and Robert A. Gross to present an early version of this essay at the College of William & Mary, and also thanks Professors Paul Boyer and John D. Ibson for their assistance.

1. Adam Moss, "Catcher Comes of Age," *Esquire*, December 1981, p. 57; Jack Salzman, ed., intro. to *New Essays on "The Catcher in the Rye"* (New York: Cambridge University Press, 1991), pp. 6, 7.

2. Salzman, intro. to *New Essays*, pp. 6, 19 n. 16; Ian Hamilton, *In Search of J.D. Salinger* (New York: Random House, 1988), p. 136; Moss, "Catcher Comes of Age," pp. 56, 57; [Jack Skow,] "Invisible Man," in *Salinger: A Critical and Personal Portrait*, ed. Henry Anatole Grunwald (New York: Pocket Books, 1963), p. 4.

3. David J. Burrows, "Allie and Phoebe" (1969), reprinted in *Holden Caulfield*, ed. Harold Bloom (New York: Chelsea House, 1990), p. 80; Hamilton, *In Search of Salinger*, pp. 155-56.

4. Salzman, intro. to *New Essays*, p. 22 n. 46; [Skow,] "Invisible Man," p. 4; Moss, "Catcher Comes of Age," p. 57.

5. Quoted by Nadine Brozan, "J.D. Salinger Receives an Apology for an Award," *New York Times*, 27 April 1991, p. 26.

6. Stefan Kanfer, "Holden Today: Still in the Rye," *Time*, 7 February 1972, pp. 50-51.

7. J.D. Salinger, *The Catcher in the Rye* (Boston: Little, Brown, 1951), p. 171. Subsequent page references, enclosed in parentheses in text, are to this edition.

8. Shawn Levy, *King of Comedy: The Life and Art of Jerry Lewis* (New York: St. Martin's, 1996), p. 271; Peter Shaw, "Love and Death in Catcher in the Rye," in *New Essays*, p. 100.

9. John Fowles, *The Collector* (Boston: Little, Brown, 1963), pp. 156-57, 192, 219-20, 246; John Simon, *Private Screenings* (New York: Macmillan, 1967), p. 165.

10. Priscilla Johnson McMillan, "An Assassin's Portrait," *New Republic*, 12 July 1982, pp. 16-18.

11. Moss, "Catcher Comes of Age," p. 58; Daniel M. Stashower, "On First Looking into Chapman's Holden: Speculations on a Murder," *American Scholar* 52 (Summer 1983): 373-77; Jack Jones, *Let Me Take You Down:*

Inside the Mind of Mark David Chapman, the Man Who Killed John Lennon (New York: Villard Books, 1992), pp. 7, 22, 17479, 184; Warren French, *J.D. Salinger, Revisited* (Boston: Twayne, 1988), pp. 17, 48.

12. Richard Schickel, *Intimate Strangers: The Culture of Celebrity* (Garden City, N.Y.: Doubleday, 1985), p. 280; Lincoln Caplan, *The Insanity Defense and the Trial of John W. Hinckley, Jr.* (Boston: David R. Godine, 1984), pp. 42-43.

13. John Guare, *Six Degrees of Separation* (New York: Random House, 1990), pp. 31-35, 107.

14. Quoted by Justin Kaplan, in *Mr. Clemens and Mark Twain* (New York: Simon & Schuster, 1966), pp. 268-69.

15. Frank Trippett, "The Growing Battle of the Books," *Time*, 19 January 1981, p. 85; Mary Jordan, "Reports of Censorship in U.S. Schools Up 50%," *International Herald Tribune*, 4 September 1992, p. 5.

16. Quoted by Salzman, in intro. to *New Essays*, p. 15.

17. Quoted in Salzman, intro. to *New Essays*, p. 15; Pamela Steinle, "'If a Body Catch a Body': *The Catcher in the Rye* Censorship Debate as Expression of Nuclear Culture," in *Popular Culture and Political Change in Modern America*, ed. Ronald Edsforth and Larry Bennett (Albany: State University of New York Press, 1991), p. 127; L. B. Woods, *A Decade of Censorship in America: The Threat to Classrooms and Libraries, 1966-1975* (Metuchen, N.J.: Scarecrow Press, 1979), p. 82.

18. Quoted by Seth Mydans, in "In a Small Town, a Battle Over a Book," *New York Times*, 3 September 1989, p. 22; Woods, *Decade of Censorship*, p. 150.

19. "Catcher in the News," *Esquire*, December 1981, p. 58; Salzman, intro. to *New Essays*, p. 14.

20. Quoted by Edward B. Jenkinson, in *Censors in the Classroom: The Mind Benders* (Carbondale: Southern Illinois University Press, 1979), p. 35.

21. Jenkinson, *Censors in the Classroom*, pp. 35, 156; Jack R. Sublette, *J.D. Salinger: An Annotated Bibliography, 1938-1981* (New York: Garland, 1984), pp. 160, 162, 164-67.

22. Marvin Laser and Norman Fruman, "Not Suitable for Temple City," in *Studies in J.D. Salinger: Reviews, Essays, and Critiques*, ed. Laser and Fruman (New York: Odyssey Press, 1963), pp. 124-29.

23. Mydans, "Small Town," p. 3.

24. Mydans, "Small Town," p. 3.

25. Willie Morris, "Houston's Superpatriots," *Harper's*, October 1961, p. 50; Laser and Fruman, Community Critics... and Censors, in *Studies in Salinger*, p. 123.

26. Leslie A. Fiedler, *Being Busted* (New York: Stein & Day, 1969), pp. 59, 60; Edward Allen, *Mustang Sally* (New York: W. W. Norton, 1992), pp. 20-21; Anna Quindlen, "Don't Read This," *New York Times*, 1 October 1994, sec. 4, p. 23.

27. Timothy Noah, "Censors Right and Left," *New Republic*, 28 February 1981, p. 12.

28. Robert J. Clements, "Forbidden Books and Christian Reunion," *Columbia University Forum* (Summer 1963): 28; Conversation with Jonas Barciauskas, librarian for theology, Boston College, 28 October 1996.

29. Warren Hinckle, *If You Have a Lemon, Make Lemonade* (New York: Bantam Books, 1976), pp. 41-42, 44-45; Robert O. Bowen, "The Salinger Syndrome: Charity Against Whom?" *Ramparts*, May 1962, pp. 52-60.

30. Robert Harris, *Fatherland* (London: Hutchinson, 1992), p. 17; Robert Darnton, *Berlin Journal, 1989-1990* (New York: W. W. Norton, 1991), p. 205.

31. Woods, *Decade of Censorship*, pp. 149-50.

32. Quoted by Mydans, in "Small Town," p. 22; "Censorship's Coming of Age," *Boston Globe*, 3 September 1993, p. 14.

33. Carol and Richard Ohmann, "Reviewers, Critics, and *The Catcher in the Rye*," *Critical Inquiry* 3 (Autumn 1976): 34-36.

34. John Seelye, "Holden in the Museum," in *New Essays*, pp. 24, 32.

35. Charles A. Reich, *The Greening of America* (New York: Random House, 1970), pp. 222-23.

36. E. L. Doctorow, *The Book of Daniel* (New York: Random House, 1971), p. 95.

37. Tom Hayden, *Reunion: A Memoir* (New York: Random House, 1988), pp. 8-9, 17-18.

38. Roland Marchand, "Visions of Classlessness, Quests for Dominion: American Popular Culture, 194S1960," in *Reshaping America: Society and Institutions, 1945-1960*, ed. Robert H. Bremner and Gary W. Reichard (Columbus: Ohio State University Press, 1982), pp. 179, 181-82.

39. John Updike, "Franny and Zooey," in *Salinger: A Portrait*, pp. 58-59.

40. Paul Levine, "J.D. Salinger: The Development of a Misfit Hero,"

Twentieth-Century Literature 4 (October 1958): 97, reprinted in *If You Really Want to Know: A Catcher Casebook*, ed. Malcolm M. Marsden (Chicago: Scott, Foresman, 1963), p. 48; and "The Fiction of the Fifties: Alienation and Beyond," in *America in the Fifties*, ed. Anne R. Clauss (Copenhagen: University of Copenhagen, 1978), pp. 46-49; Kenneth Keniston, *The Uncommitted: Alienated Youth in American Society* (New York: Harcourt, Brace & World, 1965), pp. 7-8.

41. Jack Newfield, *A Prophetic Minority* (New York: Signet, 1967), pp. 28-29.

42. [Skow,] "Invisible Man," in *Salinger: A Portrait*, p. 5; David Riesman, with Nathan Glazer and Reuel Denney, *The Lonely Crowd: A Study of the Changing American Character*, abr. ed. (Garden City, N.Y.: Doubleday Anchor, 1953), pp. 278-82; French, Salinger, Revisited, pp. 57-58; James Lundquist, *J.D. Salinger* (New York: Ungar, 1979), pp 657.

43. T. Morris Longstreth, "New Novels in the News," in *Christian Science Monitor*, 19 July 1951, p. 7, reprinted in If You Really Want to Know, p. 6.

44. Robert A. Gross, review of *Making of a Counter Culture*, in *Newsweek*, 15 September 1969, p. 98; Theodore Roszak, *The Making of a Counter Culture: Reflections on the Technocratic Society and Its Youthful Opposition* (Garden City, N.Y.: Doubleday Anchor, 1969), p. 174n; Grunwald, intro. to *Salinger: A Portrait*, p. xxx.

45. Alan Nadel, *Containment Culture: American Narratives, Postmodernism, and the Atomic Age* (Durham, N.C.: Duke University Press, 1995), pp. 71, 75, 79, 86, 181; "Communist Infiltration of the Motion Picture Industry," in *Thirty Years of Treason*, ed. Eric Bentley (New York: Viking, 1971), p. 149.

46. "The Complete J.D. Salinger," *Esquire*, December 1981, p. 58; Hamilton, *In Search of Salinger*, pp. 13-14.

47. Eve Horowitz, *Plain Jane* (New York: Random House, 1992), pp. 52, 200, 230.

48. David Riesman and Evelyn Thompson Riesman, *Conversations in Japan: Modernization, Politics, and Culture* (New York: Basic Books, 1967), p. 171.

49. John Hohenberg, *The Pulitzer Prizes* (New York: Columbia University Press, 1974), pp. 19, 55-56.

50. Hannah Arendt, *Eichmann in Jerusalem: A Report on the Banality of Evil*, rev. ed. (New York: Viking, 1964), p. 49; Vladimir Nabokov to John

Leonard, 29 September 1971, in *Nabokov's Selected Letters*, 1940-1977, ed. Dmitri Nabokov and Matthew J. Bruccoli (San Diego: Harcourt Brace Jovanovich, 1989), p. 492.

51. Longstreth, "New Novels," pp. 5-6.

52. Julie Lasky, "Savage Puritans Ripped Her Bodice," *New York Times Book Review*, 12 November 1995, p. 67; Walter Lippmann, "The Nature of the Battle over Censorship" (1927), in *Men of Destiny* (Seattle: University of Washington Press, 1970), pp. 100-102.

53. Steinle, "If a Body," p. 136.

54. Steinle, "If a Body," p. 136; Seelye, "Holden in the Museum," p. 29, and *The True Adventures of Huckleberry Finn* (Evanston, Ill.: Northwestern University Press, 1970), p. 339.

55. Lippmann, "Nature of the Battle over Censorship," p. 99.

56. Quoted by Charles Rembar, in *The End of Obscenity* (New York: Random House, 1968), p. 156.

57. The absenteeism of Holden's parents is noted perceptively by Jonathan Baumbach, in The *Landscape of Nightmare* (New York: New York University Press, 1965), p. 65.

58. Quoted by Sanford Pinsker, in *Bearing the Bad News: Contemporary American Literature and Culture* (Iowa City: University of Iowa Press, 1990), p. 29.

59. Hamilton, *In Search of Salinger*, p. 4; Moss, "Catcher Comes of Age," p. 56.

60. Steinle, "If a Body," p. 131.

61. Quoted by Nat Hentoff, in *Free Speech for Me—But Not for Thee: How the American Left and Right Relentlessly Censor Each Other* (New York: HarperCollins, 1992), pp. 374-75.

62. Quoted by Joan DelFattore, in *What Johnny Shouldn't Read: Textbook Censorship in America* (New Haven: Yale University Press, 1992), p. 109.

63. June Edwards, "Censorship in the Schools: What's Moral about *The Catcher in the Rye?" English Journal* 72 (April 1983): 42.

64. Quoted by Salzman, in intro. to *New Essays*, pp. 5-6; Edward P. J. Corbett, "Raise High the Barriers, Censors," *America*, 7 January 1961, pp. 441-42, reprinted in *If You Really Want to Know*, pp. 68-70.

65. Riley Hughes, "New Novels," *Catholic World*, November 1951, p. 154, reprinted in *Holden Caulfield*, p. 8; Moss, "Catcher Comes of Age," p. 56; Steinle, "If a Body," p. 129; Quindlen, "Don't Read This," p. 23; Hentoff, *Free Speech for Me*, pp. 374-75.

66. French, *Salinger, Revisited*, p. 42.

67. Thomas Doherty, *Projections of War: Hollywood, American Culture, and World War II* (New York: Columbia University Press, 1993), pp. 54, 56; Hilary Mills, *Mailer: A Biography* (New York: Empire Books, 1982), pp. 90-93; *Rembar, End of Obscenity*, p. 17n; Noel Perrin, *Dr. Bowdler's Legacy: A History of Expurgated Books in England and America* (New York: Atheneum, 1969), p. 251.

68. Quoted by Rembar, in End of Obscenity, p. 7; Walter L. Hixson, *Parting the Curtain: Propaganda, Culture, and the Cold War, 1945-1961* (New York: St. Martin's, 1997), p. 123; "The Third Debate," 13 October 1960, in *The Great Debates: Background, Perspective, Effects,* ed. *Sidney Kraus* (Bloomington: Indiana University Press, 1962), p. 397.

69. Gerald Rosen, "A Retrospective Look at *The Catcher in the Rye*," *American Quarterly* 29 (Winter 1977): 548, 557-58.

70. Perrin, *Dr. Bowdler's Legacy*, pp. 8, 105, 163, 167-72, 212, 220.

Chronology

1919   Jerome David Salinger is born on January 1, in New York city, to Solomon and Miriam Jillich Salinger.

1932   Enrolled in McBurney School, Manhattan.

1934   Enters Valley Forge Military Academy in Pennsylvania.

1936   Graduates from Valley Forge Military Academy.

1937   Travels to Europe.

1938   Briefly attends Ursinus College, Collegeville, Pennsylvania.

1939   Attends a short story writing course taught by Whit Burnett at Columbia University. His first short story, "The Young Folks," is published the following year in Whit Burnett's magazine, *Story*.

1942   Drafted into United States Army and attends Officers, First Sergeants, and Instructors School of Signal Corps.

1943   Stationed in Nashville, Tennessee, then transferred to the Army Counter-Intelligence Corps. Short story "The Varioni Brothers" published in the *Saturday Evening Post*.

1944   Sent to Europe, assigned to the Fourth Division of the U.S. Army and later lands at Utah Beach as part of the D-Day invasion force. Participates in European campaigns as Security Agent for the Twelfth Infantry Regiment.

1945   Marries first wife, Sylvia.

1945–47   Discharged from Army in 1945 and begins to publish regularly in the *Saturday Evening Post*, *Esquire*, and the *New Yorker.*

1948–50   Begins long publishing relationship with the *New Yorker*; publishes the major short stories "A Perfect Day for Bananafish," "Uncle Wiggily in Connecticut," "Just Before the War with the Eskimos," "The Laughing Man," and "For Esmé—With Love and Squalor" in the *New Yorker* during these years.

1950   The film version of "Uncle Wiggily in Connecticut," *My Foolish Heart*, is released by Samuel Goldwyn and stars Susan Hayward and Dana Andrews.

1951   *The Catcher in the Rye* published. "Pretty Mouth and Green My Eyes" published in the *New Yorker.*

1953   Moves to Cornish, New Hampshire. "Teddy" published in the *New Yorker*; *Nine Stories* published in April.

1955   Marries Claire Douglas on February 17; "Raise High the Roof Beam, Carpenters" and "Franny" are published in the *New Yorker*. A daughter, Margaret Ann, is born on December 10.

1957-59   "Zooey" and "Seymour: An Introduction" are published in the *New Yorker.*

1960   Son Matthew is born on February 13.

1961   *Franny and Zooey* published.

1963   *Raise High the Roof Beam, Carpenters and Seymour: An Introduction* published.

1965   "Hapworth 16, 1924" published in the *New Yorker.*

1967   Divorced from Claire.

1974   Salinger denounces the unauthorized *The Complete Uncollected Short Stories of J.D. Salinger* in his only public statement in many years.

1986   Files suit against San Francisco booksellers over a pirated collection of short stories.

1987   Publication of Ian Hamilton's biography, *J.D. Salinger: A*

Writing Life, is prohibited because quotations from Salinger's letters violate his copyright.

1997   *Hapworth 16, 1924* reportedly to be republished in the form of a book.

Works by J.D. Salinger

Catcher in the Rye. Boston: Little, Brown, July 1951.

Nine Stories. Boston: Little, Brown, April 1953.

Franny and Zooey. Boston: Little, Brown, September 1961.

Raise High the Roof Beam, Carpenters and Seymour: An Introduction. Boston: Little, Brown, 1963.

Hapworth 16, 1924. Alexandria, VA: Orchises Press. (Publication date uncertain.)

Works about J.D. Salinger

Alexander, Paul. *Salinger: A Biography*. Los Angeles: Renaissance Books, 1999.

Alsen, Eberhard. "Raise High the Roofbeam, Carpenters' and the Amateur Reader," *Studies in Short Fiction* 17:39-47, 1980.

Bidney, Martin. "The Aestheticist Epiphanies of J.D. Salinger: Bright-hued Circles, Spheres, and Patches; 'Elemental Joy and Pain,' " *Style* 34:117-131, 2000.

Bloom, Harold, ed. *J.D. Salinger: Modern Critical Views*. Philadelphia: Chelsea House Publishers, 1987.

_____. *J.D. Salinger's* The Catcher in the Rye. Philadelphia: Chelsea House Publishers, 1996.

_____. *J.D. Salinger*. Philadelphia: Chelsea House Publishers, 1999.

Boorstin, Daniel. *The Americans*. New York: Random House, 1965.

Bryan, James. "The Admiral and Her Sailor in Salinger's 'Down at the Dinghy,'" *Studies in Short Fiction* 17:174-178, 1980.

_____. "The Psychological Structure of *The Catcher in the Rye*." *PMLA* 89:1065-1074, 1974.

Cohen, Hubert I. "'A Woeful Agony Which Forced Me to Begin My Tale': *The Catcher in the Rye*." *Modern Fiction Studies* 12:335-366, 1966-1967.

Coles, Robert. "A Reconsideration of J.D. Salinger." *New Republic*, 28:30-32, April 1973.

Dahl, James. "What about Andolini?" *Notes on Contemporary Literature* 13:9-10, 1983.

Engel, Steven, ed. *Readings on The Catcher in the Rye.* San Diego, CA: Greenhaven Press, 1998.

French, Warren. *J.D. Salinger, Revisited.* New York: Twayne, 1988.

Goldstein, Bernice and Sanford Goldstein. "Ego and 'Hapworth 16, 1924." *Renascence* 24:159-167, 1972.

_____. " ' Seymour: An Introduction':Writing as Discovery." *Studies in Short Fiction* 7:248-256, 1970.

_____. "Zen and *Nine Stories.*" *Renascence* 22:44-55, 1970.

Gross, T.L. "J.D. Salinger: Suicide and Survival in the Modern World." *The South Atlantic Quarterly* 68:452-462, 19962.

Grunwald, Henry Anatole, ed. *Salinger, A Critical and Personal Portrait.* New York: Harper & Row, 1962.

Hamilton, Ian. *A Search for J.D. Salinger.* New York: Random House, 1988.

Kirschner, Paul. "Salinger and His Society: The Pattern of Nine Stories." *London Review* 6:34-54, 1969.

Lettis, Richard. "Holden Caulfield: Salinger's 'Ironic Amalgam.'" *American Notes & Queries* 15: 43-45, 1976.

Lundquist, James. *J.D. Salinger.* New York: Ungar, 1979.

Miller, James E. Jr. *J.D. Salinger.* Minneapolis: University of Minnesota Press, 1965.

Mitchell, Susan K. " 'To Tell You the Truth....' " *CLA Journal* 36:145-156, 1992-1993.

Pattanaik, Dipti R. " 'The Holy Refusal': A Vedantic Interpretation of J.D. Salinger's Silence." *Melus* 23 (1998): 113-128, 1998.

Pinsker, Sanford. *The Catcher in the Rye: Innocence Under Pressure.* New York: Twayne, 1993.

Purcell, William F. "Narrative Voice in J.D. Salinger's 'Both Parties Concerned' And 'I'm Going Crazy." *Studies in Short Fiction* 33.2:278-280, 1998.

Rosen, Gerald. "A Retrospective Look at *The Catcher in the Rye.*" *American Quarterly* 29: 547-562, 1977.

_____. *Zen in the Art of J.D. Salinger.* Berkeley, CA: Creative Arts Books Co., 1977.

Salinger, Margaret A. *Dream Catcher: A Memoir*. New York: Washington Square Press, 2000.

Salzberg, Joel, ed. *Critical essays on Salinger's* The Catcher in the Rye. Boston: G.K. Hall, 1990.

Salzman, Jack, ed. *New Essays on* The Catcher in the Rye. New York: Cambridege University Press, 1991.

Silverburg, Mark. "A Bouquet of Empty Brackets: Author-Function and the search for J.D. Salinger." *Dalhousie Review* 75:222-246, Summer-Fall 1995.

Tierce, Mike. "Salinger's 'De Daumier-Smith's Blue Period.'" *The Explicator* 42(no. 1): 56-58, 1983.

Wenke, John. *J.D. Salinger:A Study of the Short Fiction*. Boston: Twayne, 1991.

Whitfield, Stephen J. Cherished and Cursed: Toward a Social History of *The Catcher in the Rye. The New England Quarterly* 70:567-600, 1997.

Zapf, Hubert. "Logical Action in *The Catcher in the Rye*." *College Literature* 12:266-271, 1985.

WEB SITES

http://members.ols.net/~ernieh/HuertgenForest.html

http://partners.nytimes.com/books/98/09/13/specials/salinger-speaks.html

http://partners.nytimes.com/books/98/09/13/specials/salinger-sequel.html

http://www.rutherford.org/fuf/fuf-print.asp *Mark David Chapman*

http://www.amazon.com/exec/obidos/ASIN/0914061658/jonradel/105-1176539-8861512 *Amazon.com page regarding Salinger's upcoming book.*

Contributors

HAROLD BLOOM is Sterling Professor of the Humanities at Yale University and Henry W. and Albert A. Berg Professor of English at the New York University Graduate School. He is the author of over 20 books, including *Shelly's Mythmaking* (1959), *The Visionary Company* (1961), *Blake's Apocalypse* (1963), *Yeats* (1970), *A Map of Misreading* (1975), *Kabbalah and Criticism* (1975), *Agon: Toward a Theory of Revisionism* (1982), *The American Religion* (1992), *The Western Canon* (1994), and *Omens of Millennium: The Gnosis of Angels, Dreams, and Resurrection* (1996). *The Anxiety of Influence* (1973) sets forth Professor Bloom's provocative theory of the literary relationships between the great writers and their predecessors. His most recent books include *Shakespeare: The Invention of the Human*, a 1998 National Book Award finalist, and *How to Read and Why*, which was published in 2000. In 1999, Professor Bloom received the prestigious American Academy of Arts and Letters Gold Medal for Criticism.

NORMA JEAN LUTZ, is a freelance writer who lives in Tulsa, Oklahoma. She is the author of more than 250 short stories and articles as well as over 50 books of fiction and non-fiction.

ALFRED KAZIN was a noted critic and cultural historian. He has written many books on American literature and culture and was a member of the American Academy of Arts and Sciences. His works include *On Native Grounds* (1942), *An American Procession* (1984), and *God & the American Writer* (1997).

CLIFFORD MILLS is a freelance writer and editor, and formerly an editor at John Wiley and Sons.

STEPHEN J. WHITFIELD holds the Max Richter Chair in American Civilization at Brandeis University. His works include *A Death in the Delta: The Story of Emmett Till* (1988), *The Culture of the Cold War* (1991, rev. and expanded ed. 1996), and *In Search of American Jewish Culture* (1999).

Index